CONCENTRATION IN MODERN INDUSTRY

CONCENTRATION IN MODERN INDUSTRY

Theory, measurement and the U.K. experience

Leslie Hannah and J. A. Kay

First published 1977 by
THE MACMILLAN PRESS LTD
London and Basingstoke
Associated companies in New York
Dublin Melbourne Johannesburg and Madras

ISBN 0 333 19082 3

Printed in Great Britain by
BILLING AND SONS LTD
Guildford, Worcester and London

338.8
H243c

78-6332

'I wish the Roman people had but a single neck!'
The tyrant Caligula, cited by Suetonius (120)

Contents

Acknowledgements

Many people have helped us with this work. Our principal debt is to George Richardson, who persuaded both of us that industrial economics was a worthwhile subject of study: we hope that this does something to persuade him that this is a worthwhile branch of it. We are indebted to Margaret Ackrill, who prepared the populations and estimates of firm sizes for 1919, 1930 and 1948; and to Keith Walker for similar work on the modern merger statistics. Their work was undertaken with financial support from the Social Science Research Council. We are grateful to S. Aaronovitch, M. C. Sawyer, the Department of Industry and T. A. Wells and the staff of the Monopolies Commission for supplying us with data. Clive Payne wrote our computer programmes. P. E. Hart, M. A. King, D. S. Lane, R. I. McKibbin and S. J. Prais made helpful comments on earlier drafts. We have also benefited from discussions of these and related issues with many people, and would particularly mention A. B. Atkinson, J. S. Flemming, W. P. Kennedy, J. A. Mirrlees and W. J. Reader. The views expressed here are our own: and if any of the mistakes are theirs (which is improbable) the responsibility for them is ours. Blame for Chapters 1, 3, 5 and 8 should in the first instance be addressed to Hannah; and for Chapters 2, 4, 6 and 7 to Kay; but since we have in the main convinced each other that the agreed version published here is right, we hope that we shall also persuade the reader.

L. Hannah
Emmanuel College, Cambridge

J. A. Kay
St. John's College, Oxford

List of Figures and Tables

Readers' Guide

This book is somewhat uneven in style and content. We are dealing here with a topic whose analysis requires the use of statistical tools and economic theory, but whose importance is largely derived from social and political factors which have little to do with the normal subject matter of economics. If we have been at all successful in our aim of covering these diverse aspects of the growth of industrial concentration, different parts of what we have written will be of interest to different groups of readers, and our objective here is to steer each to appropriate sections within the book. Broadly, the general reader who is principally concerned with everyday policy implications of the increasing dominance of large corporations, and who is willing to take the details of our economic analysis on trust, will wish to read Chapter 1, pp. 18 to 22 of Chapter 2, Chapter 3 and Chapter 8. If he does so, he will manage to avoid all our mathematics and most of our statistics, and he will be reading a volume which is – intentionally – a good deal more polemical in tone than the book as a whole.

The second group of readers we have in mind are students with a few days to ascertain the major issues involved in the subject of industrial concentration. We hope that they will find some assistance in Chapters 2, 3 and 4. While the mathematical level of these sections is not particularly demanding, there are rather more symbols scattered around these pages than appear in most texts on industrial economics. We have tried to give sufficiently detailed literary explanations of what we are doing to enable the reader who skips lightly over these sections to grasp the essentials of what is being said: but the non-mathematical reader whose assignment really has to be written for tomorrow might be permitted to abandon Chapter 4 after the section on 'unsatisfactory measures of concentration' provided he subsequently glances at pp. 61 to 63. If there is more time to pursue some of the issues we raise, the analysis of the opening sections of Chapter 2 is in a similar spirit to that of Shubik (1959) and Telser (1972), though the latter is not easy reading. Good surveys of the empirical literature on the relationship between market structure and prices are to be found in Collins and Preston (1968) and in Weiss (1971). An introduction to the sociological literature on size and industrial relations is given by Child (1969), while extracts from many of the principal writings on bureaucracy can be found in Merton (1952). Useful economic analyses of bureaucratic behaviour are those of Downs (1967) and

Niskanen (1973). The discussion of Chapter 4 is not, we think, paralleled elsewhere. A comprehensive if somewhat tedious exposition of the problems of using empirical data to study market concentration is contained in Evely and Little (1960). One of the best discussions of the issues involved in choice of measure is still that of Adelman (1951); the line of argument of Hall and Tideman (1967) is somewhat similar in spirit to that developed here. Some readers will wish to see the parallel approach to measurement and ranking problems of Rothschild and Stiglitz (1970) and for income inequality by Atkinson (1970) and Kolm (1969), though the argument of the latter is extremely difficult to follow.

But we would not have written this book if we did not think we also had things to say to our professional colleagues, and for them the main original material in the book is in Chapters 4–7. Chapter 4 contains a systematic axiomatic approach to the choice of concentration measure; Chapters 5 and 6 describe our empirical findings on the growth of concentration in the U.K. between 1919 and 1976; and Chapter 7 discusses the 'Gibrat effect' from both theoretical and empirical viewpoints. Nevertheless, we hope that industrial economists will also read what we have to say in Chapters 2 and 3. The information we use there is derived entirely from secondary sources, but it has been our endeavour to provide a relatively fresh approach, which stresses the need to base the economic appraisal of concentration more firmly in economic theory while at the same time it seeks to broaden the somewhat narrow perspective in which economists have tended to view what we believe is one of the most important political issues of the present day.

1 Large Firms in Modern Industry

At the beginning of this century, the hundred largest firms in British manufacturing industry controlled about 15% of its net output. The biggest of these was J. and P. Coats, which had net assets of £5·5m and employed 5000 workers. The share of output held by the top hundred companies now approaches 50%. A measure of the change which has occurred can be obtained by looking at one of the smallest of these 1975 giants. Scottish and Newcastle Breweries, for example, employs 27,500 people, sells output worth £200m annually, and holds assets to the value of £150m. The largest U.K. manufacturer, Imperial Chemical Industries, has 200,000 employees and assets in excess of £2000m. The principal concern of this book is this increasing concentration of control over industrial capital – and hence over output, sales and employment – by large corporations.

It is widely believed that this dramatic growth in the power and impact of large organisations is an inevitable product of modern technology and large-scale output. Our primary purpose in this volume is to analyse the way in which this growth in concentration has come about in modern manufacturing industry. We show that it is almost wholly due to merger; that without the benefit of their acquisitions large firms would not have grown more rapidly than small. There may be intrinsic advantages which large firms systematically have and their competitors lack, but if the major one is the power to use their greater financial resources to buy other firms, the real advantage to the economy of their dominance may be minimal. It is not, we think, an accident that Britain, which combines a highly developed securities market with negligible legal restrictions on merger, has achieved increases in and levels of concentration which are the highest among developed countries with large and diversified economies. While we cannot prove counterfactual propositions, the evidence we shall present makes it difficult to believe that increases in concentration on the scale of those which we describe could have occurred if there had been substantial obstacles to amalgamation and if public policy had been hostile to these developments rather than acquiescent or encouraging.

If these changes in industrial structure are not inevitable, it makes sense to ask if they are desirable, and an important area for debate is opened up. We cannot succeed here in reaching firm conclusions on this question, which involves a wide range of considerations in which legal, political and social aspects are as important as the economic. But we shall seek to set out some of the issues for that debate, since in our view the focus of the extensive economic discussion of concentration has been excessively narrow.

The roots of the changes we describe lie in the later nineteenth century. At that time, there occurred the first intense wave of merger activity among firms which created a number of large corporations, some of which – like Vickers and English Calico – remain among the leading firms of their sector, though their recent performance has often been less dynamic. Alfred Marshall was an early witness of these developments and already in the first edition of his *Principles of Economics* (1890, p. 376) he foresaw that

> The struggle between the solid strength of the steady-going firms with large capitals on the one hand, and the quick inventiveness and energy, the suppleness and variation of smaller rivals on the other, seems inclined to issue in the large majority of cases in the victory of the former.

though it was not until the sixth edition (1910) that he was convinced that the development of joint stock companies in the mergers of these two decades had tilted the balance decisively in the direction of the large company. The trend towards larger firms which he observed has continued with little interruption, as can be seen from the solid line in Figure 1.1. Industrial concentration increased rapidly in the 1920s, and after a lull in the depression of the 1930s and the Second World War, a rapid rise was sustained in the long period of postwar expansion. Correspondingly, the role of small firms has been substantially reduced in recent years. In 1935, there were 136,000 firms which employed less than 200 people, accounting for 35 % of output, but by 1963 their number has diminished by more than half, and the 60,000 which remained shared only 16 % of output (Bolton Committee 1971, pp. 59–60). Compared with other industrial countries, and contrary to widespread popular myth, Britain now appears to have a relatively weak complement of small firms. Even within the remaining small firm sector the influence of larger organisations is substantial; over a third of small manufacturing enterprises sell a quarter or more of their output to only one customer (Davies and Kelly 1971). Similar trends towards larger firms are observable in all major industrial countries. The merger wave of the nineteen sixties – which was a major factor behind the rising concentration shown in Figure 1.1 – appears to have been a world-wide phenomenon. (Ryden 1972, De Jong 1971). In the past and in the short

term, however, substantial differences have arisen between countries. In
the United States, the share of the largest 100 firms in manufacturing
output (see the dotted line in Figure 1.1) has risen from a somewhat
higher level than in Britain in the early years of the present century, a
level which was no doubt due to the more intensive merger wave
experienced in the U.S.A. at the turn of the century (Hannah 1974a).
More recently, however, the pace of advance has slowed down in the
U.S.A., probably as a result of the increasing stringency of antitrust law
enforcement in that country, and the share of the largest 100 firms is now
lower there than in Britain.

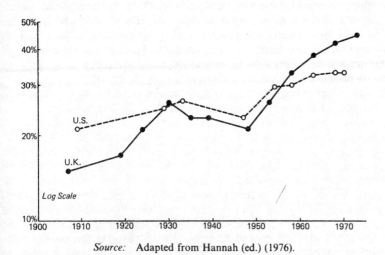

Source: Adapted from Hannah (ed.) (1976).

Fig. 1.1. The share of the largest 100 firms in manufacturing net output in the
U.K. and U.S., 1907–73

Comparison with other European countries is more difficult, partly
because of differing census definitions of firms (subsidiaries for example
are usually classed separately from their parent companies in European
censuses) and partly because of the traditions of greater bank involvement in the finances and management of industrial undertakings in
countries such as Germany and Belgium, coupled with less stringent
disclosure requirements, which together create considerable difficulties
in disentangling the precise structure of control of industry in those
countries from published company data. Nonetheless it seems clear that
in Germany, a country with a very similar industrial economy to
Britain's, initial progress towards increasing the scale of enterprise was,
as in America, more rapid than in Britain (Brady 1933). After the war the
allied occupying powers attempted to break down high levels of
concentration in some sectors (as they did also in Japan) and, although

concentration has recently increased further, the share of large firms is still somewhat lower in Germany than it is in Britain (Prais and Reid 1974). Indeed Britain appears recently to have been developing large scale firms more rapidly than other European countries. Measuring the size of a firm by the total number of its employees (whether they are employed in the domestic economy or abroad) there were in 1972 as many as 30 British companies with 40,000 or more employees, compared with only 12 each in Germany and France, 6 in Italy, 5 in the Benelux countries and 3 each in Switzerland and Sweden (Prais and Reid 1974). Britain is, then, an especially interesting country in which to study industrial concentration in that, not only is she more heavily in-dustrialised than most countries, but she has experienced more in-tensively than others the process which we examine. This is not, of course, to say that Britain's large firms are the largest or even the most numerous. In America there were at least 89 firms employing 40,000 or more people in 1972, more than in all European countries put together, but that was at least as much a result of the large size of the American economy as it was of the dominance of the large firms within it.

Whilst local or short-term factors – the history of merger activity, the size of markets, the pace of technical diffusion and so on – may lead to differences in the size of large firms and in industrial concentration between countries at any point in time, the general long-term trend in all countries is unmistakable: the importance of small firms has been reduced and large firms have produced an increasing share of industrial output. In Britain – and, in so far as we are able to judge from published data, in most other countries also – this is partly a consequence of the competitive extinction of small firms in their battle in the market place with larger, or otherwise more efficient firms; but it also arises from the direct absorption by large firms of their smaller rivals. Acquisition and merger have been closely associated with the rises in concentration which have occurred, and we will suggest (Chapters 5 and 6 below) that mergers have in fact been the major cause of the rise in concentration in Britain, at least among firms for which data is available. The process of con-centration through merger has been gradual and cumulative as is evident from the examination of the history of almost any large corporation. Figure 1.2, for example, shows the historical antecedents of the present day General Electric Company in the form of a genealogical tree. This shows only the more important mergers of G.E.C. and its constituent companies – there were many other small ones – but it is obvious even from this partial view that the modern company – which dominates the British electrical engineering industry – owes its origins to many firms acquired over the years. The process culminated in 1967–8 when G.E.C. (with 1967 sales totalling only £180 million) used its reputation for high profitability and efficient management to win the support of both government and stock market and took over its two larger rivals, A.E.I.

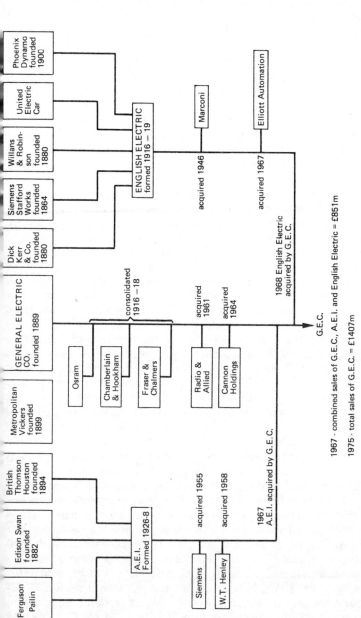

Fig. 1.2. Antecedents of G.E.C.

1967 - combined sales of G.E.C., A.E.I. and English Electric = £851m

1975 - total sales of G.E.C. = £1407m

(1967 sales: £260m) and English Electric (1967 sales: £411m) (Jones and Marriott 1970). G.E.C. is not untypical: British Leyland, Allied Breweries and many major companies would show similar family trees with branches as prolific as those of a royal house, and even firms which have recently been relatively inactive or unsuccessful as acquirers often have a considerable background of merger activity in their past. Imperial Chemical Industries, for example, the largest British company in manufacturing industry, can trace its origins to a merger of the four largest firms in the chemical industry in 1926. Over the last century – the equivalent of only four human generations – its ancestors, those once independent firms which have now found their way into the divisions and subsidiaries of I.C.I., number more than six hundred (Reader 1970 and 1975).

Mergers can very rapidly increase the size of a firm – G.E.C. more than quadrupled its sales within a year by acquiring A.E.I. and English Electric – but, whilst this may offer the quickest way of growing, it is by no means the only (nor necessarily the most profitable or socially beneficial) route to larger scale. The building of new factories and the creation of new markets – usually called 'internal' growth to distinguish it from 'external' growth by merger – also plays a major role, though this process of organic growth is normally a more gradual element. It has nevertheless been a substantial factor in the growth of most large companies and, for the economy considered as a whole, it is, of course, the only path to economic growth. An important source of I.C.I.'s expansion, for example, has been its large expenditure on research and development, which has enabled the firm to invest in a range of new products such as polythene or, through purchase of U.S. technology, nylon. In the motorcar industry, also, Ford owe their dominant position largely to continuous internal investment at Dagenham. In some industries in which the product or process is new – as with the introduction of mass production methods at Dagenham in the 1930s – internal growth will be the only worthwhile source of expansion open to the firm. In the postwar years, Xerox (through Rank Xerox in Britain) and I.B.M. have grown very rapidly internally to achieve dominant positions in the copying and computer industries. In cases like these, it is American subsidiaries or licensees – assisted by their access to the technology and skills of their American parents – which have grown rapidly by internal means and this reflects the early lead which U.S. corporations gained over their European counterparts in organising modern, science-based mass-production industries. (Chandler 1962, Servan-Schreiber 1969). However, historically British firms like Courtaulds and Morris Motors have also experienced rapid internal growth, and more recently there have been firms like Ready Mixed Concrete and International Computers, both now leading firms and strongly dependent on internal growth.

Large firms may achieve dominant positions through confidence and skill in investment in internal growth or in acquisition, but it is not always the case that large firms prosper. The two largest products of the 1967–8 merger boom – G.E.C. and British Leyland – developed in very different ways thereafter. G.E.C. achieved effective rationalisation and substantial and continuing growth in profits, whereas British Leyland suffered rapid erosion of its competitive position and was ultimately saved from liquidation only by nationalisation. Upper Clyde Shipbuilders demonstrated that amalgamations of companies with uncertain prospects do not necessarily achieve greater security, and absorbed substantial government aid before going spectacularly bankrupt. Grand Metropolitan transformed itself from a small private hotel company to a firm with assets comparable in value to those of G.E.C. by means of a chain of expensive acquisitions, but failed to maintain confidence in its management or financial structure and saw its shares depreciate in value by 90% within three years. But in both the U.S. and Britain there is considerable stability among the leaders and atrophy is a more common fate for ill-managed giants than collapse. Vickers and A.E.I. are outstanding instances of companies which achieved large size through amalgamations and subsequently went through lengthy periods of stagnation. Table 1.1 shows both the stability and the mobility of industrial giants. Six of the ten largest companies of 1957 remain in the top ten of 1969, and these six – I.C.I. Unilever, Imperial Tobacco, Courtaulds, Distillers and G.K.N. – were all also among the top ten of 1930. Four have however dropped out, sluggish performers pushed out by firms which had enjoyed rapid expansion – principally through merger – during the 1960s. Bowater, Vickers, Esso (U.K.) and Dunlop had been replaced by G.E.C., British Leyland, Bass Charrington and Allied Breweries.

This size mobility among the leaders is of more particular interest in that it illustrates an important principle in the evolution of high levels of concentration: that, even if the largest firms in the economy do not grow more rapidly than their competitors, concentration may nonetheless still increase. The ten large firms of 1957 listed in Table 1.1 had grown substantially by 1969 but in that year, as the second column of figures shows, they still controlled much the same proportion of manufacturing assets – about a quarter – as they had in the earlier year. Yet over the period the share of the ten largest firms had increased (third column) – an apparent paradox which is easily resolved by noting that the composition of the top ten has altered. This effect – which we call the Gibrat effect after the French economist who first drew attention to the phenomenon (Gibrat 1931) – may be likened in operation to the process of natural selection in the theory of evolution. In any period some firms of all size classes will do well and some will do badly. This dispersion in performance induces a steady increase in the dispersion of the distribution of firms' sizes, which could imply a secular upward trend in concentration, even if there were no systematic tendency for large firms to grow more rapidly than small ones.

TABLE 1.1 Large firms in U.K. manufacturing industry 1957–69

The ten largest companies in 1957[a]			The ten largest companies in 1969	
	Assets £m 1957	Assets £m 1969		Assets £m 1969
1. I.C.I.	545	1427	1. I.C.I.	1427
2. Unilever	309	479	2. G.E.C.	691
3. Imperial Tobacco	205	466	3. Unilever	479
4. Courtaulds	169	442	4. Imperial Tobacco	466
5. Bowater	144	262	5. Courtaulds	442
6. G.K.N.	138	294	6. British Leyland	328
7. Distillers	125	317	7. Allied Breweries	318
8. Vickers	120	103	8. Distillers	317
9. Esso	116	274	9. Bass Charrington	314
10. Dunlop	113	258	10. G.K.N.	294
Total top ten	1984	4322		5076
Total, all manufacturing companies	8090[b]	17773		17773
Ten as % of total	24·5	24·3		28·6

Notes: [a] The 1957 top ten excludes Steel Co. of Wales (assets, £145m), subsequently nationalised; and A.E.I. (assets, £117m), subsequently acquired by G.E.C.
   [b] The 1957 total excludes £561m assets of subsequently nationalised steel companies.

Sources: 1957: *Studies in Company Income, Assets & Finance* (H.M.S.O. 1960)
   1969: Department of Trade and Industry.

A major objective of this book is to explore the relative importance of the Gibrat effect, and of other sources of concentration increase, in the British economy. In Chapter 4 we consider the desirable properties of a measure of industrial concentration, and evaluate against them some of the measures which have been used in the now considerable literature on this subject. We show that by these criteria some commonly used indicators are inadequate, and that satisfactory measures are systematically related to each other and capable of extension to cater for the catholic range of possible views on the dimensions of concentration. In Chapters 5 and 6 we apply this range of measures to empirical data, investigating the role of internal growth and merger in the changing levels of concentration over the past six decades in Britain. We find that concentration has indeed increased substantially over this period, primarily as a result of merger, although there have been long periods in which it has not risen and may well have declined. The Gibrat effect, and its implications for the size distribution of firms in the long run, is considered in more detail in Chapter 7. In Chapter 8 we describe some possible policy implications of our analysis. But first in Chapters 2 and 3 we evaluate more precisely what we mean by concentration and why economists, political scientists and sociologists – and politicians and citizens – should be interested in the phenomenon.

2 Concentration and Market Power

CONCENTRATION AND THE THEORY OF OLIGOPOLY

Many economists think of monopoly and competition as two polar cases, with the real world lying somewhere in between, and the degree of concentration measures whether a particular industry lies closer to one extreme or the other. The closer an industry is to the monopolistic end of the spectrum the more monopolistic characteristics will be observed, the higher prices will be relative to costs, the greater the resulting resource misallocation and welfare losses. This view has some plausibility, but it is much too vague to be considered a useful economic theory or to provide a satisfactory basis for empirical work. (This has not, however, prevented the proliferation of empirical studies in this area more or less devoid of theoretical underpinning). We must look more carefully at the ways in which high concentration might affect the relationship between prices and costs.

Under perfect competition, each firm believes its output decision will have a negligible effect on market price. Under monopoly, the firm's output decision is the principal determinant of market price. Concentrated industries lie somewhere in between in the sense that individual firms will have some, but incomplete, influence on price but because of the interdependence of the decisions of different firms the intermediate case is much more complex than either of the extremes. Faced with this difficulty, the most common reaction of the industrial economist has been to despair, mutter something about the essential indeterminacy of prices under oligopoly and continue writing his monograph on the five-firm concentration ratio. But prices are not indeterminate, as anyone who has ever been shopping has presumably discovered, and the statement that they are is merely an admission of the lack of a satisfactory theory.

The most useful recent contributions to the development of such a theory have come from the theory of games and that is the line of approach we shall pursue here. Suppose there are a small number of producers, each making a homogeneous product. Each is reasonably well informed about the production possibilities open to his competitors: we shall assume that each can produce as much as desired at constant marginal cost, although the level of cost may vary from producer to producer, with c_i the production cost for firm i. We might think of a group of small town market gardeners, of varying degrees of efficiency, dominating their local market and knowledgeable about each other's capacities. The price which they will realise for their produce will depend on the amount which, in aggregate, they grow. There is no collusion between them. Each is therefore concerned to make his own output decision, x_i, in order to maximise his own profits, given the output decisions x_j, x_k etc. which the other producers have made. But he does not know what output the others are planning and must therefore base his decision on his expectations of x_j, x_k, etc. How are these expectations to be formed? Each producer knows that the others are in a similar situation, so that firm j will be aiming at an output x_j, which maximises j's profits given his expectations of the outputs x_i, x_k etc. of all the other firms. Now suppose that we can find outputs $\bar{x}_i$, $\bar{x}_j$, $\bar{x}_k$ and so on such that $\bar{x}_i$ maximises i's profits given $\bar{x}_j$, $\bar{x}_k$ etc.; x_j maximises j's profits given $\bar{x}_i$, $\bar{x}_k$ etc.; and similarly for all other firms. In that case firms would only have an incentive to choose some different output if they did not wish to maximise profits, or if they believed that some other firms did not wish to maximise profits (or if they believed that some firms believed that some other firms did not wish to maximise profits, or that some firms believed that other firms believed that other firms did not wish to maximise profits, and so on *ad infinitum* – we can probably confine our attention to the first two or three orders of belief). These outputs $\bar{x}_i$, $\bar{x}_j$, $\bar{x}_k$ would therefore be the rational choices of profit maximising firms in a profit maximising world.

In general we can find outputs which meet these conditions. Indeed they correspond to the oldest solution to the analysis of oligopoly behaviour – the Cournot solution – in which each firm maximises its profits given the outputs of all other firms. But the arguments we have given for supposing this solution to be the likely outcome are very different from the ones expounded by Cournot and justly criticised in the majority of elementary textbooks on industrial economics. We have employed the concept of a Nash equilibrium – a solution to a non-cooperative game which obtains for each participant the maximum available pay off given the strategies of all other participants – which is relevant in a wide range of economic contexts. It is easy to see that this Nash – Cournot solution implies a positive association between prices and concentration. The smaller the proportion of total output which the rest of the industry supplies, the lower will be the elasticity of demand faced by an individual firm and the greater its capacity to raise prices and profits by limiting its own output. Since similar considerations apply to all firms, the greater the degree of concentration the greater the excess of prices over costs. Following Cowling and Waterson (1974) we can pursue this more formally by noting that we require for each firm i that

$$\frac{\partial \pi}{\partial x_i} = p - c_i + x_i \frac{\mathrm{d}p}{\mathrm{d}x} \cdot \frac{\mathrm{d}x}{\mathrm{d}x_i} = 0 \text{ with } \frac{\mathrm{d}x}{\mathrm{d}x_i} = 1$$

Multiplying through by x_i, and summing over all firms gives

$$px - \Sigma c_i x_i - px \cdot \left(-\frac{x}{p} \cdot \frac{\mathrm{d}p}{\mathrm{d}x} \right) \Sigma \left(\frac{x_i}{x} \right)^2 = 0$$

where x is aggregate output for the industry. Now $\left(-\frac{x}{p} \cdot \frac{\mathrm{d}p}{\mathrm{d}x} \right)$ is the reciprocal of the elasticity of demand, μ, and $\Sigma \left(\frac{x_i}{x} \right)^2$ is the Herfindahl index of concentration, H, which we shall discuss in more detail in Chapter 4. Rearrangement therefore gives

$$\frac{px - \Sigma c_i x_i}{px} = \frac{H}{\mu}$$

On the left we have the average price-cost margin in the industry, which will be directly and positively related to the Herfindahl concentration measure. In Chapter 4 we show that one property of this index is that its reciprocal can be thought of as representing the equivalent number of equal-sized firms in the industry. Thus the fraction of the revenue of the industry which takes the form of monopoly profit is inversely proportional to (i) the effective number of firms in the industry (ii) the elasticity of demand for the industry's product.

This model assumes a homogeneous product, so that oligopolists have no effective freedom to determine their prices: they choose quantities and accept the market-determined price. Many oligopolistic industries are characterised by some forms of product differentiation, so that individual firms can, if they wish, set and maintain prices which differ from those of their competitors. The simplest way to represent such a market is to suppose that the differentiating characteristic is location, and we shall consider the simplest form of this problem by supposing that customers have fixed demands and are arrayed at a uniform density along a line. The locational analogy need not be interpreted literally. Following Lipsey (1963) we might think of one end of the line as denoting a toothpaste irresistible to the opposite sex but ineffectual at cleaning teeth and the other one fatal to oral bacteria and sexual success alike, while intermediate positions represent intermediate combinations. Although demands are fixed each consumer always buys from the nearest firm. This leaves to each producer two decisions – where to locate (i.e. what product to manufacture) and what price to sell at. The interaction of these variables with the similar decisions of his competitors will determine the quantity he sells and the profits which result.

Define z_i as the location of firm i, measured as a distance from some

Fig. 2.1. Spatial competition

origin. Let a_i be the dividing point between the markets of firm $(i-1)$ and firm i, where the firms are labelled consecutively from the origin. Let the density of customers be 1 per unit distance, and transport costs k per unit distance. Firm i has costs c_i per unit and sets price p_i. Then we have a Nash equilibrium if p_i and z_i maximise

$$\pi = (p_i - c_i)(a_{i+1} - a_i), \text{ subject to}$$

$$p_{i-1} + k(a_i - z_{i-1}) = p_i + k(z_i - a_i) \tag{1}$$

$$p_{i+1} + k(z_{i+1} - a_{i+1}) = p_i + k(a_{i+1} - z_i) \tag{2}$$

Differentiation of (1) and (2) yields $\left\{\dfrac{\partial a_i}{\partial p_i}\right\}_{z_i} = -\left\{\dfrac{\partial a_{i+1}}{\partial p_i}\right\}_{z_i} = \dfrac{1}{2k}$

so that $\left\{\dfrac{\partial \pi}{\partial p_i}\right\}_{z_i} = (a_{i+1} - a_i) - \dfrac{1}{k}(p_i - c_i) = 0$ for maximum π (3)

If s_i is the market share of firm i and L the length of the line, then

$$s_i k L = (p_i - c_i) \tag{4}$$

so that $\displaystyle\sum_i (p_i - c_i)s_i = k L \sum_i s_i^2 = kLH$

Thus in this model the average price-cost margin per unit is proportional to the Herfindahl concentration index H. It is worth noting that this derivation does not assume that the zs are chosen to maximise profits, so that the analysis applies even for arbitrary locational choices – which might for example have been determined by historical factors and are now costly to change.

It is however interesting to consider what an equilibrium set of zs might be. To do this we will suppose that our line is in fact the circumference of a circle. We do this to avoid the minor complications involved in analysing the ends of the line. These occur because the firms occupying the most extreme positions can be sure of attracting all customers on one side of them and will therefore locate themselves as near as possible to the second firm and to the penultimate firm. This is the Principle of Minimum Differentiation, after Hotelling (1929) who first showed that with only two firms in the type of situation described here they would locate next to each other: the model purported to explain the similarity in the policies of Republican and Democrats and of I.T.V. and the B.B.C. (Steiner 1961). This aspect becomes relatively unimportant as the number of firms increases (Eaton and Lipsey 1975) and the analysis below can readily be generalised to take account of it.

There are many possible types of Nash equilibrium locational choices. This can be seen by noting that in Figure 2.1 any alternative positioning of z_i which still resulted in a_i and a_{i+1} lying in the interval (z_{i-1}, z_{i+1}) would yield the same size of market for firm i. So if z_i is a profit maximising location, so are all these others. It is not unreasonable, however, to suppose that if a firm could reduce its customers' transport costs without reducing its own profits it will do so – that it will not follow the Principle of Minimum Differentiation out of sheer perversity. So an equilibrium set of choices would be one in which, given the price and locational decisions of all other firms, each firm maximised its own profits and, subject to attaining that level of profit, minimised transport costs within its market. In the case considered here, this means that each firm will locate at the mid point of its market. The same would be true if a firm were required to pay all or any part of transport costs itself. This gives a further condition for all i that

$$(z_i - a_i) = (a_{i+1} - z_i) \tag{5}$$

Substituting this into (3) gives

$$(p_i - c_i) = 2k(a_{i+1} - z_i)$$
$$\text{and } (p_{i+1} - c_{i+1}) = 2k(z_{i+1} - a_{i+1}) \tag{6}$$

while rearrangement of (2) gives

$$(p_{i+1} - p_i) = k(a_{i+1} - z_i) - k(z_{i+1} - a_{i+1}) \tag{7}$$
$$= \tfrac{1}{3}(c_{i+1} - c_i)$$

Summing (4) over all firms gives $\Sigma(p_i - c_i) = kL$.

Thus the sum of the price-cost margins of all firms is equal to the total cost of transporting a unit of the product from one end of the market to the other. From (7)

$$p_i - p_{i-j} = \tfrac{1}{3}(c_i - c_{i-j})$$

and summation over all j gives

$$(p_i - c_i) = \frac{kL}{n} - \tfrac{2}{3}(c_i - \frac{1}{n}\sum c_i)$$

In the simplest case where all firms have the same costs of production, each will charge $\dfrac{kL}{n}$. Each firm will have the same market area, so that they are located equidistantly. Where there are cost differences between firms, one-third of each firm's divergence from the average of all firms will be passed on to consumers and the remaining two-thirds absorbed into profits. In equilibrium the price charged by firm i is determined by the costs of all other producers and therefore the price, market share and profits of each firm are the same in all possible equilibria: they can differ only in the order in which the market areas are arranged.

An interesting feature of this model is that the location of firms is efficient if they all have the same costs, but not otherwise. Consider a point on the boundary between the market areas of two firms. At such a point the cost to a consumer of buying from either firm (including transport costs) will be the same. But, because cost differences are not fully reflected in price differences, it would be cheaper to supply him from the lower cost producer. Thus the market shares of relatively low-cost producers will be too low and high-cost producers will have excessive market areas. High concentration leads not only to excessive margins between prices and costs, but also to an inefficient allocation of output between producers.

In the analysis above we were considering a single output decision by the various firms in the industry. In practice, of course, output decisions are normally made sequentially. Each producer has an opportunity to see what his rivals have done in the past and that might influence the decision he makes on his future output. Obviously this eases the informational requirements of the model: firms can learn about cost and demand conditions from the market rather than by looking over the walls of their rivals' market gardens. But, assuming all firms have acquired the relevant information, is something different from the Nash–Cournot solution now likely to occur? Superficially it would appear not. After all any departure from this solution will reduce profits, unless a rival also departs from it: and, since the same is true for him, it is unlikely that he will. But it has been shown that excess profits depend on the degree of concentration and hence are less under oligopoly than under pure monopoly. Thus total industry profits are below their potential maximum and if *all* firms were to restrict output *all* firms could earn increased profits thereby. It is important to realise the instability of such an arrangement. It requires each firm to refrain continuously from maximising its own profits in the interests of the industry as a whole.

If we are considering a single output decision, there can be no possible incentive for a firm to do such a thing. If the game is played only once, the rational strategy for all firms to follow is to produce the Cournot output and this is the right thing for all to do even though all are aware that they would earn greater profits if they all produced less. This paradox, known as the Prisoner's Dilemma, recurs in many economic contexts: an outstanding exposition is to be found in Luce and Raiffa (1957). If the game is played again, however, a firm may be induced to attend to group rather than selfish interests by the threat of subsequent punishment. This 'punishment' will have to take the form of other firms expanding their output and reducing its profits to the Nash–Cournot level – or worse, if rivals are ready to sacrifice their own profits in order to inflict damage on an offender (and each other) – for some lengthy or indefinite period thereafter. A firm will be tempted to cheat if it thinks that it may be able to do so without being detected, or if it is pessimistic about the prospects of the cartel's survival (since there are advantages in being the first to cheat). The extent of such pessimism is in turn likely to hinge on the probability of detection, since this will be the principal influence on other firms' decision to cheat.

Thus the likelihood that a cartel will succeed depends, in general, on the ease with which violation of its understandings can be observed and punished. Until now it has not been important to distinguish between formal cartels, with a central organisation and written agreements, from informal arrangements in which there is no communication between participants other than a mutual recognition of self-interest. But, in the context of policing, the nature of the agreement is crucial and we consider informal ones here: formal arrangements are outlawed in the U.S. and more or less outlawed in the U.K. and many other countries. If there is no central information office issuing instructions, then firms will only be able to observe and react to their own experience. With a homogeneous product the announced price of all the cartel members will necessarily be the same and each participating member will expect to obtain a certain market share at that price. Since this will be below the output which would maximise individual profits, each firm will be tempted to sell more by offering some under the counter discount, improvement on standard specification or similar device. Other firms will discover this when they find it difficult to sell their allocated share at the agreed cartel price. They will then feel justified in employing these methods themselves to increase their own share; these sales will be won at the expense of other firms who may react similarly and the cartel will be subject to gradual attrition which would be likely to culminate in a bout of overt price cutting.

Firms' actual sales are likely to deviate from their allocated sales even if cheating does not occur because of errors in the estimation of market demand and chance elements entering the behaviour of buyers. This raises an immediate problem for implicit collusion in unconcentrated industries, since random fluctuations in sales of this kind are likely to be relatively much greater for small firms than for large. If firms will be satisfied with the cartel's operations if they obtain – say – 90% of their expected sales, then small firms are more likely to be dissatisfied than large. Suppose there are n customers each buying the same amount, and all have probability s_i of purchasing from firm i. The firm i will expect to obtain a market share s_i, and the variance of that share will be $\frac{s_i}{n}\left(1 - s_i\right)$. The likelihood of obtaining a given proportion of the market will depend on the magnitude of the standard deviation of market share relative to the mean, i.e. on $\sqrt{\frac{1}{n}\left\{\frac{1}{s_i} - 1\right\}}$. It is easy to check that this will fall with s_i, and is three times as great for a firm with market share of 10 % as for one with 50 %. However firms may realise this and smaller firms show a greater tolerance than large before concluding that the cartel under- standings are being violated. They might, for example, be willing to adhere to the agreement until their sales were so low that the probability of this occurring by chance was below (say) 5 %. In this case the chance that any firm will (wrongly) conclude the rules of the game are being violated will be the same, but the unconcentrated industry will still be at a disadvantage simply because of the larger number of firms who may draw this conclusion. But it probably does not matter if some in- significant firms think they are being cheated. We might suppose that the cartel could survive unless firms with total market share greater than some figure s thought they were being cheated.

Suppose each firm sets its level of minimum expected sales such that the probability of being provoked into retaliatory action is p. Then, if its intended share is s_i, the amount which it will contribute to the group of disaffected firms is s_i with probability p, and zero with probability $(1-p)$. Thus the expected value of its contribution is ps_i and the variance $p(s_i -ps_i)^2 +(1-p)(ps_i)^2 = p(1-p)s_i^2$. Summing this over all firms the fraction of all firms which are likely to be dissatisfied with the cartel has mean p and variance $p(1-p)\Sigma s_i^2$. If there are a reasonable number of firms in the industry, the probability of the critical level s being exceeded will depend on the variance of this distribution, which we note is proportional to Σs_i^2, the Herfindahl concentration index introduced earlier. Thus we can expect the extent of dissatisfaction with the operation of the cartel, and the likelihood of its successful continuance, to depend on the existence of a sufficiently high level of concentration as measured by this index.

We can now draw the threads of this discussion together and try to summarise the nature of the relationship between concentration and price-cost margins suggested by oligopoly theory. Three quite different arguments have suggested that the most useful indicator of con- centration is likely to be the Herfindahl measure. We should not attach too much weight to this conclusion since the models we have developed are very simple ones: but it is interesting to note that, as we shall show in Chapter 4, this indicator stands out among others in being heavily influenced by the sizes of the largest firms in the industry and is relatively insensitive to the presence or absence of a smaller competitive fringe. At low levels of concentration there will be a non-cooperative situation in which the relationship between concentration and price-cost margins will be approximately linear. At some sufficiently high level of con- centration, however, the implicitly collusive outcome becomes feasible. Here there is likely to be a sharp jump in prices as a shift from the Cournot solution to the joint profit maximising solution occurs. Further increases in concentration will not lead to further increases in profits.

Thus we expect a relation which is linear over part of the range with a subsequent discontinuity. In practice, of course, things will not be as clear cut as this. There will be some difference between industries in the level of concentration which permits collusion and it is possible that, where collusion is under strain, prices will not be pushed as high as a monopolist might attempt. (Although such restraint reduces the incentive to cheat, it also reduces the incentive to participate.)

THE EMPIRICAL EVIDENCE

There is now a very large number of empirical studies of the relationship between concentration and profits or price-cost margins, mostly American. These have been surveyed in some detail by Collins and Preston (1968) and by Weiss (1971), to which we refer the reader, emphasising here only those which are relevant to our main arguments. This work provides overwhelming evidence for the view that high levels of concentration are associated with relatively high levels of profits. The relationship is not a particularly strong one, however, in two senses. Increases in concentration do not imply very large increases in prices: Collins and Preston (1968) suggest that a 10 % increase in the four firm concentration ratio might imply an increase in prices of between 1 % and $1\frac{1}{2}$% and this is not out of line with the orders of magnitude implied by other estimates. Nor do variations in the degree of concentration explain a large part of interindustry or intertemporal variations in profits. Neither of these observations should surprise us. The kinds of measures of concentration which empirical economists are normally forced to use (most commonly 3-, 4-, or 5- firm concentration ratios) are rather poor approximations in several respects to the measures which our theory requires – the difficulties involved in the practical measurement of concentration in general and of market concentration in particular are discussed at length in Chapter 4. Nor is there anything in our arguments to suggest that the existence of market power in oligopolistic industries will prevent the existence of substantial differences in profitability between firms and between industries as a result of differences in efficiency, fortune and the economic environment in which they operate.

The pioneering study of the concentration/profit rate relation was that of Bain (1951) who examined data for a range of industries and suggested that there was a discontinuity observable, with industries in which the largest eight firms held a market share in excess of 70 % earning markedly higher returns. The majority of subsequent studies have used regression analysis and implicitly assumed that a continuous linear relationship is the appropriate one. A number of authors have further examined the possibility of a dichotomous relationship. Kilpatrick (1967) finds levels of and changes in profit rates related to both concentration ratios and to a dummy variable reflecting whether or not a critical level of concentration is exceeded, but the former relationship is more marked. Collins and Preston (1968) also found evidence for both, while concluding that a continuous relation was more generally applicable. Meehan and Duchesneau (1973) attempted perhaps the most systematic exploration of this issue and came down in favour of Bain's hypothesis. All these writers, however, have regarded the two possibilities as alternatives: the oligopoly theory we have outlined suggests that we would expect to observe both a continuous relationship and a discrete break, so that the observations are complementary rather than contradictory. Some support for this can be obtained from the findings of Telser (1972) who estimates the concentration – profit relationship for observations stratified into 'low', 'medium' and 'high' concentration industries. He finds evidence of discontinuity, with a higher and more significant regression coefficient in the 'high' concentration group. Although our theory suggests that above the point at which collusion becomes feasible the relation between profits and concentration will become weaker rather than stronger, Telser's results are those which we should expect to observe when the break in the relationship is only approximately identified (as is likely to be the case when 'high concentration' is defined by a four firm concentration ratio of 50 %): a group defined in this way is likely to contain some industries with Cournot outcomes and others with joint profit maximising solutions and an (imperfect) tendency for the latter to be associated with the higher values of the concentration ratio. Thus we may conclude that the American evidence is consistent with the view of oligopoly which we have outlined.

There are many fewer British studies and their results are more equivocal. An early one was that of Hart (1968, pp. 258–264) who found only a weak relation between concentration and profits. Holtermann (1973) and Khalilzadeh-Shirazi (1974) suggested it was negligible although the latter finds a simple correlation which disappears in multivariate analysis. But the concentration measure which they use is a weighted average of the concentration ratios relating to the products of the industry. It is not easy to see what such a figure means and it certainly cannot be interpreted as a concentration ratio for the industry as a whole, with which it is in fact rather poorly correlated (see Boyle 1973; Metcalf and Nickell 1975). Khalilzadeh-Shirazi does find that profits are significantly related to a variable based on the ratio of the median size plant to the total industry output. This seems to us a rather poor barrier-to-entry variable – these surely depend on absolute rather than relative capital requirements – and may perhaps be more sensibly interpreted as an approximate indicator of concentration. Certainly we do not regard either of these studies as inconsistent with the findings of Cowling and Waterson (1974) who do find the anticipated relationship in one of the few studies to use the Herfindahl index which we have suggested is appropriate. These results acquire support from the very different approach of Metcalf and Nickell (1975).

It seems that the correlation between concentration and high profits is less marked in the U.K. than in the U.S., but there are a number of reasons why we might expect this to be so. Monopoly confers on firms a greater freedom to pursue objectives which increase the welfare of managers and it does not seem implausible that differences in social attitudes in the two countries imply that the pursuit of profitability contributes less to managerial utility on this side of the Atlantic. British managers may be more susceptible to Hicks' dictum that 'the best of all monopoly profits is a quiet life' (Hicks 1935). It is also possible that British firms are more diversified, thus blurring the significance of a relation between concentration in an industry and the profits of firms. This hypothesis finds some support in the evidence of Sutherland (1969) who collates the findings of a number of Monopolies Commission studies showing that firms whose activities are investigated earn higher profit rates on the goods which are the subject of the reference than they do on their business as a whole. Finally the British economy is more susceptible to penetration by imports than the American so that concentration ratios will be an especially poor measure of market shares in Britain. Only the last of these explanations is one from which we can derive reassurance in the context of the econometric results reported for the U.K. that concentration does not lead to the exaction of excessive profits.

THE ORIGINS OF MONOPOLY PROFITS

If we accept that high profit rates and high concentration are found together, some problems of interpretation remain. It is possible that large market shares confer monopoly power on firms with no other special advantages: it is also likely that some firms possess particular capabilities or technologies which enable them to achieve both market dominance and above-average profits so that the latter simply represent the deserved rewards of superior performance. Thus Kelloggs and Kodak defended their position before the Monopolies Commission by arguing – with some justice – that they made nicer cornflakes and better colour film than their competitors. It is obviously important for policy purposes to distinguish these situations from monopoly abuses, since the dissolution of concentration will be detrimental in one case and beneficial in the other. This may not be easy, especially since both factors may well be present – there is no reason why firms which achieve dominance through superior efficiency should refrain from exploiting it and the Cournot model outlined earlier illustrates both these factors at work. Demsetz (1973) suggests we may discriminate by examining the relative performance of small and large firms. If concentrated industries report higher profits because of monopolistic elements, we should expect small firms to make profits as great or greater than their larger rivals: if differences in relative efficiencies are the key, then the large firms would be more profitable than the small. He shows that, in American industries, large firms tend to be more profitable than small and the difference is substantially greater in concentrated industries, concluding that reductions in concentration would be likely to have adverse consequences.

We are not, however, persuaded that the exercise of monopoly power will necessarily imply higher profit rates for small firms. First, one of the adverse consequences of oligopolistic pricing is likely to be that the exit of inefficient, high-cost producers is retarded: thus we may observe more relatively unprofitable small producers in such cases. And second, a situation in which small firms can earn above average profit rates cannot be an equilibrium one. It would be rapidly followed by the entry of many new small firms with consequent reductions in the level of concentration and the profits of firms of all sizes. At any time we should expect to observe some disequilibria of precisely this kind. But, if a monopoly is to be sustained, it is necessary that barriers to entry should either exist – in which case small firms are likely to be unprofitable – or be created by an implicit or explicit threat to cut prices on any lines produced by a new entrant. In either case the profit rates of small firms will be low and, while it is not necessary (though it is likely) that they will be lower than those of larger firms in the same industry, they will certainly be lower than those of large firms in concentrated industries generally.

Decisive tests to discriminate between benign and malignant concentration are therefore hard to find and we can do no more than suggest some other snippets of evidence. If technical superiority is the normal route to large size, then we should expect to find some general tendency for large firms to earn higher profit rates than small, whether we look at concentrated or unconcentrated industries. It appears that in the U.S. they do (Demsetz 1973; Hall and Weiss 1967), but in the U.K. they do not (Samuels and Smyth 1968; Singh and Whittington 1968). Given the role of large American companies in the development and dissemination of new technology, this is perhaps not too surprising – indeed a number of relatively small British companies are in fact the subsidiaries of U.S. multinationals whose especial capabilities may earn them high profits in both countries. It also fits into the pattern determined by an American legal structure which is hostile to merger as a route to market dominance and a British framework in which concentration increase is overwhelmingly attributable to merger.

Another possible measure of the performance of large and small British companies is the extent of their success in world markets. The results are shown in Table 2.1 and are rather startling: the firms in the largest size category export 10% of their output which compares with

TABLE 2.1. Exports as a percentage of turnover (1973)

Industry	Range of turnover (£m)						All
	250+	*100–250*	*50–100*	*25–50*	*10–25*	*<10*	
Food, drink, tobacco	3·9	3·4	3·9	7·4	3·8	4·8	4·0
Chemicals	13·5	18·6	17·3	14·6	19·7	22·9	14·9
Engineering	15·2	21·9	23·4	18·2	16·6	22·3	18·4
Ships and vehicles	27·4	38·1	22·2	17·7	14·4	11·8	26·8
Other metal goods	11·8	6·2	11·2	8·6	11·4	13·4	11·0
Textiles, footwear, clothing	19·4	11·1	14·6	9·7	11·5	11·9	14·7
Other manufacturing	4·0	7·1	8·8	14·6	9·7	11·5	7·2
All manufacturing	10·0	14·5	15·2	13·7	12·2	14·5	11·7

(Companies in sample whose accounts are analysed by Department of Trade and Industry: source D.T.I.)

14·5% for the smallest size category and 11·7% for the sample of companies as a whole. This is partly explained by industrial composition: in particular large companies are strongly represented in food, drink and tobacco industries in which both large and small firms export relatively little. Nevertheless the breakdown by industry still suggests that any relationship between size and exports is negative rather than positive. This is not very favourable to the view that size, profitability and technical superiority are associated. It does not, however, support the view that large firms are exerting monopoly power by restricting supply to the domestic market (or any other plausible theory we can construct. A partial explanation may be that large firms are more likely to own foreign subsidiaries, and supply through them rather than by direct export. The welfare economics of this is difficult to assess.)

We have shown that high levels of concentration do confer on producers the power to raise prices and profits and there is evidence that this power is exercised. Where market dominance arises from superior technical efficiency, this poses a dilemma for public policy: where it is pursued for its own sake, the implications are clear. It is therefore important to establish how high levels of concentration have come about and that is the principal subject we examine in Chapters 5 and 6.

3 The Social and Political Effects of Concentration

The economic effects of large-scale enterprise and industrial concentration have been the subject of extensive discussion, but the political and social aspects remain relatively neglected. This cannot be due to their lack of intrinsic significance. On the contrary the political and social ramifications of increasing scale are probably the most important, and some of the problems which large corporations create in the economic sphere may be better understood if we widen our analysis beyond the theory of markets to examine their impact on the internal organisation of the firm and its workforce and on political decision making in our ostensibly pluralist economy.

Economists who have studied scale economies have given priority to economic and technological factors, playing down in their work the social effects of large scale operations. An exception was Marx who felt that the attitudes created by large-scale organisation were an important factor in the alienation of industrial workers (in a pioneer survey of 1880 he drew up a questionnaire which recognised that among the factors shaping worker attitudes was the size of plants in which they worked) (Blauner 1960). Of course, as Marx saw, wage labour itself implied some loss of individual autonomy (irrespective of the size of plant) and large scale was therefore not, to Marx, the essence of alienation. In the twentieth century the conditions in many large plants have been ameliorated but it is likely that plant size remains an important determinant of worker attitudes. It is a truism that attachments in small units tend to generate reciprocated social relations and give rise to personal satisfactions and a sense of identity: people are wanted 'for themselves'. Some small firms which try to develop an intimate family atmosphere may also to some extent provide such a framework. Larger groups and large firms, by contrast, require organisation of a more formal kind and such collectivities often generate hierarchical, bureaucratic tendencies which may reduce personal initiative and participation and individual satisfaction; relationships become instrumental. In many areas of life such sacrifices are accepted because of the advantages of large scale and a commitment to collective norms. But in the work situation the conflict between the desire for economic reward from large-scale organisations and the dislike of the work experience they offer is a real and continuing one. The evidence on wage differentials strongly suggests that workers still view very large enterprises with conspicuous lack of enthusiasm (see Table 3.1). There appears to be a marked preference among workers for small firms (especially those with less than 250 employees) so that large firms have to offer wages and other employee benefits more than 25 % higher than small firms in order to attract workers. Similar relationships have been found in other countries (Kleiman 1971; Lester 1967; Masters 1969).

TABLE 3.1 Labour costs by size of firm in Britain (1968)

	Total Labour Costs, in d. per hour		
	Firms with 25–249 employees	Firms with 250–999 employees	Firms with 1000 or more employees
Food, drink and tobacco	117·70	116·44	139·80
Chemicals and allied industries	135·26	161·93	191·62
Metal Manufacture	128·35	141·14	146·77
Engineering and electrical goods	130·72	138·15	148·44
Shipbuilding and marine engineering	126·30	131·79	137·25
Vehicles	129·30	145·50	165·93
Metal goods n.e.s.	116·38	126·88	139·83
Textiles	100·72	111·47	125·72
Clothing and Footwear	93·72	93·57	103·63
Bricks, pottery, glass, cement etc.	122·96	133·23	143·96
Timber, furniture etc.	119·92	134·01	144·69
Paper, printing and publishing	134·94	138·66	164·48
Other manufacturing industries	106·84	124·24	145·38
All manufacturing industries	118·66	130·04	151·31

Source: Department of Employment, *Labour Costs in Great Britain, 1968* (H.M.S.O. 1971), pp. 30–2.

There are a number of alternative explanations for this relationship between the size of firm and labour costs. Since large firms are more capital-intensive they perhaps need more skilled labour and the differential could simply be a skill differential. Large firms are also more likely to have some monopoly power. It might be argued that this ought to enable them to restrict output (and employment) and use their monopolistic power to force down wages. Perhaps more plausible, however, – and certainly more consonant with the evidence in Table 3.1–is the view that unions are able by bargaining to obtain for workers part of the monopoly profit of dominant firms. There is support for this view in the American econometric evidence (Weiss 1966) which suggests that highly concentrated industries do tend to pay higher wages and are thereby enabled to employ staff of somewhat higher quality than average. The ability of large firms to reap economies of scale might also enable them to pay higher wages and other employee benefits.

However, given the existence of a reasonable degree of competition between workers for jobs, it is unlikely‧– except in a few industries where apprenticeship rules or other restrictions on entry effectively ration access to jobs – that these factors themselves account for differences of the magnitude shown in Table 3.1 and this suspicion is confirmed by interview studies. In a survey of firms in Bradford, for example, Ingham (Ingham 1970 Chapter 8) found that a common reply to the question 'Supposing you were looking for a job, what would be your most important consideration?' in large firms was 'money', but that in small firms only 4–9 % of workers volunteered only 'economic' reasons, many indicating that they liked work in their firm because of its interest, friendly social or management relationships, proximity to their homes or some other 'non-economic' rewards. The link between non-monetary work satisfaction and plant size may, of course, be only an indirect one. It seems clear, for example, that the loss of control over the speed or quality of work by assembly line workers (and in other technologies in which the division of labour has reduced the skill and responsibility content of jobs) created dissatisfaction, but there is no *necessary* connection between such technologies and large scale plants and firms (Woodward 1958). However these technologies are often characterised by economies of scale in practice and thus it is hardly surprising that large firms experience these problems more commonly than small (Talacchi 1960). In large firms, also, impersonal management controls and bureaucratis- ation will inevitably develop and will decrease job satisfaction. It is thus perhaps not surprising that statistical studies of the 'size effect' on employees' morale have tended to confirm the interpretation that small firms offer a more intrinsically satisfying work experience. Absenteeism is significantly more common in larger plants and firms than in small (Acton Society Trust 1953, 1957; Revans 1958; Talacchi 1960; Indik 1965) and some authors have suggested that labour turnover is higher in large firms despite the higher wages they offer (Kerr 1949; Cleland 1955). Recent evidence does not, however, support this proposition (Stoikov and Raimon 1968, Bailey 1973). It is clear, however, that large plants are significantly more strike-prone both in America (Cleland 1955) and, as Table 3.2 shows, in Britain. Almost one hundred and fifty times more working days are lost proportionately in strikes at plants in the largest size category (1000 + employees) than in the smallest (11–24 employees) and strike-proneness seems to be a continuously increasing function of size. Employee dissatisfaction may, moreover, extend beyond the shop floor and the level of the plant, for large organisations require functional specialisation in management and a larger number of hierarchical levels of authority. Increasingly, therefore, supervisory, clerical and manage- ment staff feel themselves being treated as a group rather than as individuals and job satisfaction there also declines. Middle class employees are now likely to see themselves as the instruments – rather than the controllers – of others and it is thus perhaps no accident that 'white collar' unionism has spread more rapidly in large organisations than in small (Bain 1970).

TABLE 3.2. Incidence of stoppages by size of plant 1971–3

Plant Size	Annual average no. of stoppages per 100,000 employees	Annual average no. of working days lost per 1000 employees
11– 24	8·0	14·8
25– 99	19·2	72·4
100–199	23·0	155·0
200–499	25·4	329·1
500–999	29·7	719·4
1000 +	28·7	2046·1

Source: 'The Incidence of Industrial Stoppages in the UK', *Department of Employment Gazette*, February, 1976, p. 116.

If we are to relate this analysis to quantitative measures of concentration, we should consider ways in which it might be more formally expressed. Suppose that the span of control – the number of subordinates whom any particular individual can supervise – is much the same at all levels in an organisational hierarchy: let it be x. The number of individuals in the organisation is n, so that the number of levels will be j where

$$n = 1 + x + x^2 + \ldots + x^j$$

Since $n = \dfrac{x^{j+1} - 1}{x - 1}$, $\log n + \log (x - 1) \simeq (j + 1)\log x$

$j \simeq \dfrac{\log n}{\log x}$, so that the number of tiers in the hierarchy is roughly proportional to the log of the number of members. Alienation, in the sense of labour being instrumental and not the creative expression of the worker, is likely to be related to the length of this chain of command. The degree of alienation experienced by any individual within it might depend on the number of direct superiors he has: if so, the average number of superiors A would be given by

$$nA = x + 2x^2 + 3x^3 + \ldots \qquad + jx^j$$
$$nA(x - 1) = jx^{j+1} - n + 1$$
$$= j\{n(x - 1) + 1\} - (n - 1).$$

Thus $A \simeq j - \dfrac{1}{x-1}$, so that for a given span of control x we can write $A = b + c\log n$.

These arguments suggest that an appropriate statistical measure of alienation in an organisation might be the log of the size of the organisation. There is some empirical evidence for this: Revans (1958) and Ingham (1970) compare the incidence of absenteeism with plant size and find a logarithmic relationship holds and a similar pattern is shown by the data of Table 3.2 above. Suppose an industry contains N employees, organised in firms of size n_i, then the degree of alienation A_i in firm i will be

$$A_i = b + c\log n_i$$

$$\Sigma A_i n_i = bN + c\Sigma n_i \log \frac{n_i}{N} + cN\log N$$

$$\frac{\Sigma A_i n_i}{N} = b + c\log N + c\sum \frac{n_i}{N}\log \frac{n_i}{N}$$

The first two terms of this expression indicate the maximum possible level of alienation in the industry, which depends on the size of the industry and which reaches a maximum in the case of complete monopoly. This is reduced by the third term, which is proportional to the degree of entropy in the size distribution of firms – one of the measures of concentration to be discussed below. Thus entropy is suggested as an appropriate measure of the loss of control over individual activities experienced in a hierarchical situation. Again as with economic models of oligopoly, this model is not to be taken too seriously. What is interesting is that while our economic models pointed towards the Herfindahl index as an appropriate measure of concentration, this sociologically oriented model suggests a different indicator – we believe it important to recognise that different concentration measures will be required for different purposes. Moreover as will be shown in Chapter 4, the Herfindahl index emphasises the top part of the distribution, while entropy gives weight to changes over the whole range. These models, therefore, confirm the intuitive expectation that in considering market power we are principally interested in the relative importance of the very largest firms, while the relationship between individuals and their working environment is much affected by changes in the balance between small and medium firms.

While large organisations with many hierarchical levels may be characterised by employee alienation, they are not without their attendant advantages and, indeed, those representing employee interests have tended to favour the growth of large firms. The social reformers earlier in this century, for example, when they were attempting to alleviate the appalling working conditions in East London 'sweatshops', were well aware that the most formidable barrier in their path was the extreme difficulty of enforcing protective legislation in small workshops: the conditions in those workshops provide a salutary reminder that small scale enterprise does not necessarily mean a satisfying or enriching work experience (Booth 1903). Trade union leaders have also looked favourably on the trends towards large scale bureaucratic control of business activity. Recruitment of members is more successful – Hughes (1972) reports that establishments with over 100 workers account for 63% of trade unionists but only 36% of non-unionists which may itself reflect more extensive alienation in large plants. Negotiation is easier and the power and prestige of union leaders is related to the power and prestige of those with whom they deal. Of course senior managers in large plants – spurred on by trade union pressure and by the need to prevent the scale effect impairing their overall efficiency – have been concerned to alleviate the harsher aspects of the work experience in large plants, and without the new techniques of supervision and representation which have been developed it is possible that employee dissatisfaction would have been even higher. Shorey (1975) suggests that although large plants are associated with greater susceptibility to strikes the greater development of personnel functions in large organisations implies that (for given establishment size) increase in enterprise size reduces strike activity – though his empirical evidence is indecisive. 'Job enrichment' schemes have also done something to reduce the tedium of assembly line work in a select few plants; more commonly effective supervision with acceptably sized work groups gaining some control over the processing of work at shop floor level have helped to replicate the conditions of small plants in large ones (Revans 1958). On the management side, also, the principles of decentralisation are now better understood and multi-divisional organisation, with the creation of profit centres within which individual managers can have greater autonomy and responsibility, has done something to restore a desirable sense of control (Channon 1973). It is noticeable that in an industry like chemicals – dominated by I.C.I., a large firm with large plants – indexes of employee dissatisfaction such as strike activity are below the norm for large organisations and this is no doubt partly due to the long tradition within I.C.I. of decentralised production management and progressive employee relations policies (Reader 1975; Department of Employment 1976). Even so I.C.I. itself has been sufficiently worried by the problems of large scale to consider dividing itself up into several autonomous corporations (though it decided against such a major reform (Reader 1975)); and managers in large corporations still have serious doubts about the compatibility of efficiency and large scale (Bannock 1971). The persistence of the large difference in wages necessary to attract people to work in the very largest plants – and it appears to be at the plant rather than the firm level that the work experience is most impaired by scale – suggest that the advantages of a small work environment are still worth a considerable financial sacrifice to many workers, and, even though *firms* are still growing in size, the tendency to build *plants* employing more than 1000 people appears to have been stemmed: between 1958 and 1968 the proportion of the labour force in such plants rose only slightly from 34·1 % to 34·5 % (George and Ward 1975, p. 38).

The existence of a choice between relatively well-paid work for a large organisation and somewhat less generously paid employment in a smaller (and, it appears, more intrinsically appealing) work situation does not in itself establish that an incorrect balance is being struck by society in its decisions on the scale of industry. There is considerable variation in the needs and goals of employees: all workers are not oriented towards seeking satisfying work relationships at the cost of other things; many seek their major satisfactions outside work and find that high wages enable them to attain these goals. A study of workers in various firms in Luton showed that car assemblers were distinguished from other groups by their exclusive emphasis on financial factors as influences on their employment choices – 'It's money every time. I sell my labour to the highest bidder – and around here, that's Vauxhall', is described as a characteristic comment (Goldthorpe *et al.* 1970, p. 28). But if large firms can pay the wage differentials required to attract workers so oriented and still remain profitable in a competitive environment, it is implicit that there must be compensating cost advantages to large-scale organisation. If this is so, and there is a reasonable degree of choice available to workers, then the differential wages paid by large organisations will be a tolerably accurate reflection of individual preferences between the costs and benefits of scale and of the welfare implications of their choice. But once high concentration levels are achieved, these assumptions may cease to hold. First, large firms will be more insulated from competitive forces and better able to pass on their relatively high wages in higher prices or lower monopoly profits and, second, the choice available to workers may cease to be a real one as large firms provide for many the only available opportunities for employment appropriate to their skills.

There may, therefore, be wider implications of the power over people's lives possessed by large corporations in concentrated industries. Single firms – and even single plants – are now often large in comparison with the firms within which they are situated and, though the tragic tale of Jarrow in the 1930s – a town almost wholly dependent on one shipbuilding yard which closed down – is an extreme case (Wilkinson 1939), a local oligopoly in industrial labour markets is not uncommon. Thus when their members are made redundant trade unions now tend to direct their criticism not at the capitalist market system in general, as was formerly often the case, but at the individual corporation involved. In many cases this policy is correct: the elimination of inefficient productive capacity is now less frequently achieved through the action of bank-ruptcy in a competitive market *process*, but more commonly emanates from decisions to 'rationalise' made by a bureaucratic *organisation*. (Decisions which may or may not be similar to those which would have been imposed by market forces. Clearly the large firms are constrained in some way by the requirements to make profits and serve consumers, but their monopoly power may give them a greater discretion to diverge from decisions suggested by the market.)

The power of such firms may extend beyond the labour market, giving to the relatively few men who control them considerable influence over a wide range of social and economic options. The concentration of power in large firms reduces the effectiveness of potentially important controls by shareholders and consumers. With the divorce of ownership and control, the interests of directors and managers may diverge from those of the (more numerous) shareholders and, whilst there are factors limiting this – share ownership by managers, the threat of takeover if shareholders' interests are not sufficiently considered – the superior knowledge and expertise of the controlling group or 'technostructure' (Galbraith 1967) will tend to put effective power into their hands. This need not in itself be undesirable. Shareholders are a small proportion of the population and their interests need not coincide with social interests – if they extract high profits through monopoly power, for example. A potentially more serious allegation about the modern corporation is that it derogates from consumer sovereignty by using research to devise unnecessary products and advertising to create unnecessary wants. Thus Galbraith has argued that the power of big business in America has resulted in too great a proportion of GNP being devoted to private consumption – much of it frivolous in nature – and insufficient to public sector goods and services. In Britain, also, there have been critics of the contemporary growth of a 'bastard capitalist' culture which is strongly oriented to the executive's pursuit of rivalry and growth rather than the values of compassion, mutuality and equality which the critics believe to be more decent and humane (Samuel 1960). There is certainly some truth in these allegations about the tendency of a corporate society's culture, but they are exaggerated. The business success stories of our era have made use of modern marketing techniques, but they have used them to demonstrate their capacity to satisfy real needs with superior products: I.B.M., Xerox, Polaroid, Sony, Texas Instruments are exemplars of modern capitalism, but it is difficult to dispute the genuine nature of the demand for what they had to sell. The conspicuous failures have been those who did not or could not adapt to changes in circumstances which they were powerless to control – motor manufacturers who could neither stem nor satisfy popular requirements for smaller or more reliable cars; airlines, such as Pan American or Court Line, who could not induce travellers to pay greatly inflated fuel costs to transport their depreciated currencies abroad. The strident and repetitive demands of businessmen and financiers for restraint in public expenditure may indeed be tedious and philistine, but their power is limited by the vested interest which the public sector has in its own expansion and the growth of the share of output controlled by giant corporations has been paralleled by a similar growth in the share of output controlled by the state.

The threat to consumer sovereignty implicit in rising concentration should, then, be recognised but not exaggerated. But is there a greater threat to political sovereignty? The growth of corporate power has been a matter of recurrent concern to political commentators. Before the Second World War the New Deal antitrust campaigner, Thurman Arnold, warned that such trends would lead to the decline of political freedoms and the growth of fascism, suggesting that National Socialism was simply the logical development of the German tendency to cartelisation (Arnold 1939). Political scientists (e.g. Brady 1943) and neo-liberals (e.g. Hayek 1944) agreed that current trends in business made the threat of totalitarianism a real one and documentary evidence captured by the allied armies invading Germany added further credence to the hypothesis by showing the close involvement of firms like I.G. Farben with the fascist state. But later studies have shown beyond serious doubt that the roots of the Nazi dictatorship were to be found elsewhere (Bracher 1971).

Nonetheless the emergence of mechanisms which resemble the formal apparatus of the corporate state in peacetime Britain has given cause for concern. Certainly the spectacle of the government appearing to negotiate on tax reductions with the T.U.C. in 1976 is not an edifying one for supporters of parliamentary sovereignty. But it is easy to overestimate the practical significance of these mechanisms. The overpublicised visits of the C.B.I. and T.U.C. to Downing Street are the stuff of newspaper copy, not economic management, and the N.E.D.C. sponsored meetings to discuss 'industrial strategy' generate more rhetoric than reality. In fact both the C.B.I. and T.U.C. are bodies with little authority or control over their component units, though it suits both them and governments to assert that they have more. The C.B.I., in particular, is rarely able to arrive at a consensus among its members, far less to impose a view thus arrived at on a reluctant government. These developments may be mistaken for, or may indeed become, moves subversive of formal democratic procedures. There are certainly dangers and they are aggravated by the growth of industrial concentration, but we are not persuaded that they have yet become a major political problem.

Even if we doubt the imminence of the corporate state, there remain many important respects in which political values are shaped by the economic organisation of society. The growth of the large modern corporation enables far more power to be concentrated in the hands of a few individuals than was possible in earlier stages of capitalist development. This has been a matter of serious concern for those interested in the distribution of power within society. The desire for personal independence and control over the individual's working environment is widespread in all social classes and this creates a richness and diversity in society which has been highly prized. Thus one proponent of this view has written

> Is not that community the best, and, in the widest sense of the word, most healthy, which has the largest proportion of its citizens who have the enterprise, and energy, and initiative, to create new things and new methods for themselves, and not merely to carry out the order of somebody 'higher up' (Lothian 1930)

The weakness of this dream, as socialists frequently pointed out, was that most people in our society must take orders from somebody 'higher-up' and indeed this has always been the case. One strand of socialist thought, derived from William Morris and most clearly articulated by G.D.H. Cole (Cole 1918) has demanded that production units be sufficiently small to give individuals within it a genuine say in their organisation; but in most of this century socialist parties and trade unionists have devoted attention not to dissolving concentrations of power but to criticising its association with the private ownership of production. Thus Tawney (1964, p. 173) has claimed that 'so far from resisting the concentration of economic control, the whole tendency of democracy is to accelerate and systematise it' and he argued that freedom lay not in the abolition of economic authority but in the establishment of guarantees that it be exercised in the public interest. The problems posed by the concentration of private power were thus to be solved by its transfer to the state.

But experience of nationalisation hardly supports his optimism. There is little indication that workers in state-controlled industry either have or feel that they have significantly greater influence on their working environment than those in comparable private plants, and the social and political problems of large-scale enterprise persist in publicly owned corporations. An alternative approach has been to seek to resolve these problems by systems of employee participation. But these are largely evasions of a real dilemma. There is simply no way in which 100,000 people can be given, in any meaningful sense, a say in running a firm (or any other organisation for that matter). There are no doubt some mechanisms which are more successful than others in creating, at least for a time, the illusion that individual views are respected and considered and in this context schemes for 'industrial democracy' may have a useful role to play. The addition of trade unionists to the politicians, peers and financiers who currently make up the ranks of non-executive directors may create an impression of shared power, but it is naïve to suppose that it can be other than an illusion. Hierarchical structures and authority relationships are an inevitable concomitant of large-scale organisation, though the more discreetly they are handled the greater the efficiency of the unit is likely to be and it is arguable that more democratic structures will make large-scale organisation more politically acceptable.

The restrictions on individual freedom implicit in a hierarchical structure may have equally serious effects in stifling individual enterprise and the development of new ideas. The problems which arise **are** most evident in organisations such as government service. Since this produces, in the main, no measurable output, there are few external indicators of performance. Success or failure must, then, be judged in terms of the internal functioning of the organisation: the contribution which is made to smooth running and efficient administration. But originality and imagination are qualities which are fundamentally inimical to smooth running and efficient administration. Those whose role is to challenge established ideas are, by that fact itself, difficult people to work with and such individuals are not attracted to or successful in large bureaucratic organisations. In Weber's terms (Weber 1948) 'charismatic' authority, which is ceded voluntarily to those who demonstrate superior achievement, is replaced by bureaucratic authority derived from formal structures, length of service and paper qualifications. Thus one perceptive journalist has described the atmosphere of the British Treasury:

> men with ideas are also put off by the general atmosphere of civilised scepticism. Despite all the reforms which have already taken place they still feel that it is not done to show enthusiasm for any idea. The words 'there is nothing new under the sun' seem to be written on the walls in invisible ink ... 'Scepticism' of the Whitehall variety is a very different animal from the Cartesian doubt of the philosophers, which questions old-established assumptions as a prelude to a new synthesis. British official scepticism is more directed towards new, reforming ideas than towards accepted beliefs and is not necessarily a prelude to anything at all. (Brittan 1964, p. 33)

In this way hierarchical structures come to operate established routines with increasing skill and effectiveness, but in the process lose creativity and flexibility and possibly even a sense of direction. Thus Lord Butler observes 'the (British) Civil Service is a bit like a Rolls Royce – you know it's the best machine in the world, but you're not quite sure what to do with it. I think it's a bit too smooth: it needs rubbing up a bit' (Sampson 1965, p. 263). This machine is a striking instance of the attractions and dangers of bureaucratic organisation. It is (quite properly) internationally admired for the skill, administrative expertise and integrity of its operations. Yet it is difficult to dispute that other western countries, superficially worse governed, have in the end enjoyed a much higher quality of economic and social management. The weakness of such organisation in industrial contexts is well illustrated in Gowing's account (Gowing 1974) of the U.K. atomic weapons programme: the execution of policy was effective, while the objectives of the policy were muddled, inept and shrouded in the secrecy characteristic of bureaucracies which believe their activities too important to be communicated to those they are ostensibly intended to benefit.

Downs (1967) analyses in a more general context the way in which bureaucracies develop over time. He notes how they tend to increase their internal efficiency, while shifting their emphasis from their initial functions to ensuring the survival and growth of the bureau as an autonomous unit. As this happens more formalised rule systems are developed, and the degree of conservatism increases, while the proportion of administrative staff rises. These weaknesses are to some extent inevitable features of government organisations. Their extension to private business is more recent, but it is difficult to read the history of I.C.I., for example, (Reader 1975) without being struck by the similarities. As industry becomes more concentrated, so the points at which key decisions are taken rise to more elevated levels, systems of organisation and reporting become more elaborate and more formal and the connection between individual responsibility and outcomes becomes more remote and attenuated. Long before business of the size we now have could have been imagined, Walter Bagehot's penetrating analysis of bureaucracy set out the dangers. He saw it manned by those who

> are occupied for years in learning its forms – afterwards, for years too, in applying these forms to trifling matters. . . . Men so trained must come to think the routine of business not a means, but an end – to imagine the elaborate machinery of which they form a part, and from which they derive their dignity, to be a grand and achieved result, not a working and changeable instrument. But in a miscellaneous world, there is now one evil and now another. The very means which best helped you yesterday, may very likely be those which most impede you tomorrow – you may want to do a different thing tomorrow, and all your accumulation of means for yesterday's work is but an obstacle to all the new work . . . The truth is, that a skilled bureaucracy – a bureaucracy trained from early life to its special avocation – is, though it boasts of an appearance of science, quite inconsistent with the true principles of the art of business . . . One of the most sure principles is, that success depends on a due mixture of special and non-special minds – of minds which attend to the means, and of minds which attend to the end. (Bagehot 1867, pp. 328–30)

These problems are certain to become greater. The narrow vision and inflexibility of a hierarchical structure can be overcome if the men at its top are capable of generating sufficient ideas and enthusiasm for the organisation as a whole. Many recently created giant corporations are still run by the men or the teams who built them up and in these cases such conditions often apply. But, in the longer term, their behaviour will become modified in the directions Downs suggests and their heads will no longer be entrepreneurial spirits but men who have climbed their way up that or some other organisation in the roles described by Bagehot.

If a wise man arranged the bureau rightly in the beginning, it may run rightly a long time. But if the country be a progressive, eager, changing one, soon the bureau will either cramp improvement, or be destroyed itself. (Bagehot p. 331)

We already have some evidence of how this process can work. All too often it has been the rapidly growing and dynamic firms of the 1920s and 1930s who have been industrial laggards in the postwar era. A.E.I., Morris Motors, Woolworths, Courtaulds – these are only the most prominent among companies which were among the forward-looking, innovative firms of earlier periods, enjoying exceptional growth through internal or external expansion. Each of them has experienced lengthy spells of stagnation or decline in recent years. In early capitalist development, the second and third generations of a family-controlled firm would frequently fail to match the qualities of the first and economic performance would deteriorate. Such firms would collapse under the pressure of newer or more effective firms – the spirit of 'clogs to clogs in three generations'. But giant corporations do not die and their second and subsequent generations are not incompetent but only inflexible. The atrophy which this generates is a more pervasive because more persistent problem for the industrial structure. The need to preserve incentives towards innovation is one of which many businessmen are aware, but there is evidence that the methods of decentralised decision-making which they have attempted to introduce to preserve it have been less than perfectly effective (Channon 1973). Scherer (1970, p. 354) cites the case of Standard Oil of New Jersey, with twelve layers of management between research and development scientists and top decision-makers and no major new commercial product in 15 years.

As the process of bureaucratisation continues, the similarity between the attitudes and backgrounds of leading civil servants and businessmen increases (Nettl 1965). This can be seen on one side in the increasing concern of big business with ill-defined concepts of social responsibility and on the other in the well documented tendency of regulating agencies within governments to become pressure groups for the regulated (Bernstein 1955). This increasing *rapport* has been generally welcomed by politicians, but spectators may legitimately wonder whether a friendlier relationship between the umpire and the players will necessarily lead to an improvement in the quality of the game. Not only has business become rather like government in structure and organisation, but there has been an increasing tendency to regard individual businesses as being, at least in some respects, arms of the government.

This is a development which has gathered pace in recent years. When business is relatively small and fragmented, government must necessarily deal with it – if it deals with it at all – in the same way as it deals with individuals. This involves an essentially even-handed treatment on the basis of stated criteria, and well defined rules whose interpretation is open to appeal and challenge. As concentration has increased, this 'government of laws and not of men' has come under considerable strain in the area of industrial policy. In the 1930s some large firms succeeded in negotiating especially favourable tariff treatment for their own particular benefit (Hutchinson 1965), but this was exceptional and after the war extensions of this trend were resisted by traditionally minded civil servants (Shonfield 1965). But their resistance has been steadily eroded. It was initially undermined by the government assuming powers which were rarely, if ever, exercised, but which represented a threat to be used as bargaining counters in negotiations. The Bank of England Act gives the central bank powers to issue directives to commercial banks: such directives are never in fact made, but the tacit threat of them is used to induce banks to behave in ways which it would be almost impossible to enforce by regulation: e.g. to require them to give preference to particular categories of borrower. Monopolies legislation confers authority to enforce the recommendations of the Monopolies Commission. Such orders are rarely issued; instead negotiations occur in which firms are invited, under this cloud, to modify their actions in ways which the minister or department concerned thinks desirable. The threat of negative planning controls has also often been used – for instance to induce Rootes Motors to make a commercially disastrous decision to construct a new plant at Linwood in Scotland.

Since the early 1960s the frequency and significance of discretionary interventions and government negotiations with individual firms have increased greatly. The pattern of negotiation within the framework of controls which might, but need not if behaviour is satisfactory, be imposed has become more extensive. The existence of price control legislation has greatly increased the scope for such dealings, but there have also been other developments, such as the power conferred by the 1968 Restrictive Practices Act for the government to exempt agreements which it approves or sponsors from the scrutiny of the Restrictive Practices Court. A range of positive as well as negative inducements have been employed. Government aid to industry of a generalised kind has increased, but more striking (though smaller in total) have been discriminatory aids under which approved firms or activities are able to negotiate grants, loans or subsidies for themselves of a kind which are not necessarily available on the same terms, or at all, to others. The 1975 Industry Act provides for the institutionalisation of these increasingly frequent discussions between large firms and the government in the context of 'planning agreements'. Indeed there have been suggestions that such participation should be made compulsory (Holland 1975).

Industry has not always been a willing partner in these developments. Price control has been much disliked and it is clear that government-provided finance is very unpopular and normally, though not exclusively, sought as a last resort by unsuccessful firms or for projects of doubtful commercial viability. There is an undercurrent of resistance to the prospect of continuing discussions of corporate policy with civil servants, so that one entrepreneurially oriented large firm chairman has commented that 'some of our staff have occasionally to remind themsleves that they are there to serve the interests of the customer and not the needs of the Department of Prices and Consumer Protection'. (Grand Metropolitan 1975). But the increasing similarity of personal background and organisational structure of private and public sectors has led to a far more ready acquiescence in these trends than would otherwise have been possible. The growth of industrial concentration has not only made it possible for the government to establish close and continuing relationships with major sections of industry, but has smoothed the course of these relationships.

In our view then the more serious political problem posed by industrial concentration is not the subversion of government by business, but the subversion of business by government. We have given reasons above for thinking it improbable that the attitudes or abilities required to improve Britain's industrial performance are to be found in the Civil Service. Experience supports this. The private sector industries which have formed the most extensive relationships with government have been the aircraft and ship-building industries. The history of these relationships is well known (Select Committee 1972; Reed 1973; D.T.I. 1973) and need only be briefly recounted here. The major government sponsored aviation projects have been Concorde – now established as the least successful commercial venture in recorded history – and the RB.211 aero-engine development, whose continuing difficulties led to the liquidation of Rolls-Royce, the private firm principally involved. The leading beneficiaries of assistance in shipbuilding have been Upper Clyde Shipbuilders (which also went into liquidation and was succeeded by the marginally more successful Govan Shipbuilders) and Harland and Wolff. This latter enterprise comes close to having negative value added and should probably be more appropriately regarded as a form of social security than a commercial activity.

The showpiece of government intervention in industry has been its creation of a major British capacity in aluminium smelting (Graham 1972, Dell 1973). This was established with the aid of substantial government grants and long-term contracts for the purchase of cheap electricity. The results have been somewhat variable. Anglesey Aluminium has been a consistent lossmaker, and the chairman of R.T.Z., the consortium leader, has stated that it 'is still a very worrying problem' (Chairman's statement, 21st May 1975). The Alcan smelter had serious teething troubles, but is now relatively successful. British Aluminium's plant at Invergordon came into operation after substantial cost overruns, but major failures in the associated electricity generating capacity have required continuing government subventions which are likely over the life of the project to run into some hundreds of millions of pounds. Given this record, some modesty about the capacity of the government to promote industrial efficiency might seem in order. But like medical quacks, the government acts as if it believes that the appropriate response to the failure of its remedies is not to apply less but to apply more. A still more extensive network of industry-government discussion and selective assistance is planned. We see nothing, in principle, wrong with this: freedom for the corporation is not a fundamental right akin to freedom for the individual, and equality before the law is a good deal more cogent in its application to people than it is to firms. But there are *a priori* and empirical reasons for supposing that governments are not good at this type of activity. This is not the result of evil intentions, or even of incompetence; it is simply that the organisational structures which governments inevitably acquire do not seem well adapted to the job of running business.

Disengagement by government from some of its relations with industry and a return to a general regulatory role would be a course which might be favoured. But, as the Conservatives discovered in 1970–1, it is hardly a practicable proposal in an economy with levels of industrial concentration as high as in Britain. In such a situation events and decisions will occur which appear as simply too important for the government to ignore and such problems are equally likely to arise in the private as in the public sector. (It will be evident, therefore, that we are not discussing here the merits or demerits of public *ownership*.) If there is a single manufacturer of aero-engines (as in the case of Rolls-Royce), then the strategic implications of its collapse are unacceptable. If one firm is the principal employer in a large area (as with Upper Clyde Shipbuilders), it cannot simply be allowed to go under. The intervention which occurs may be irrational and unproductive and may in some cases reduce employment and living standards in the longer run, but the political pressures for it to occur are very great. The point is vividly illustrated by the rescue of Chrysler (U.K.) in 1975 at a time of high unemployment. When 500 jobs are lost in each of 50 firms, a government finds it relatively easy to resist pressure to act; but, when 25,000 jobs are at risk in a single enterprise, the pressures are of a different order of magnitude. Thus while there is room for different views on the value of government intervention in industry and different political parties can push it far or less far as their philosophy directs them, an increased level of such intervention is an inescapable result of high levels of concentration.

It would be wrong moreover to suppose that government intervention can never be useful. There has been some more favourable experience in continental Europe. The activities of French planners have won admiration. In Italy, state agencies succeeded in the 1950s in generating an entrepreneurial spirit which was a vitalising influence on the economy (Holland 1972), though this spirit seems to have evaporated as in time the public holding companies acquired bureaucratic characteristics of their own (Polti 1974). In Britain the most successful experiment in this field was the Industrial Reorganisation Corporation, which provided finance for a number of successful ventures, of which the creation of a viable U.K. ball-bearing manufacturer (Ransome – Hoffman – Pollard) is perhaps the most prominent. It is worth noting the distinctive features of the I.R.C.'s organisation: the number of executives never exceeded a dozen, they were mostly in their thirties, and they operated with substantial freedom from ministerial or civil service control (Young and Lowe 1974); and it was perhaps no bad thing for its reputation that it was killed before it turned itself into a more conventional part of the government machine.

There is therefore some scope for constructive government intervention, but, because much government intervention results from short-term political pressures, much of it will be at best useless. The chairman of Grand Metropolitan, cited above, was criticising recurrent discussions with government departments about the price of bread. The cost of bread is dominated by the world price of wheat, and the British government's capacity to influence that is much the same as its capacity to influence the weather. The effect of these negotiations (apart from their considerable burden on the time of senior management and civil servants) has been at most to delay some inevitable increases for short periods. They can have done nothing to enhance the economic performance of the bakery industry, but that has not been their purpose. They are what Abraham (1974) has described as 'government by cosmetics'; their object is to create an impression of activity. This is not entirely new. In the rapid inflation of 1919–20, for example, government committees were appointed under the contemporary Profiteering Acts to investigate prices, but it would have been quite impossible for them to monitor (far less control) the prices of the many competing, and typically small firms, and they did not seek to do so (Pigou 1947, pp. 127–34, 230). But with the growth of concentration the frequency of such actions has increased, and so has their impact – not necessarily in the desired or desirable directions.

A more concentrated economy is, then, one in which government is likely to have a stronger influence on the quality of the economic choices being made. Clearly a society which entrusts a high proportion of its decisions about its own future to its government (and to large corporations acting in concert with it) lays itself open to certain dangers.

Careerism and patronage can be discouraged by decentralised decision-making in which individuals take responsibility for their actions, but they are encouraged in large bureaucracies, where the criterion for performance becomes the ability to please one's superiors. A plurality of decision-makers, many of them free of government control, has therefore been considered a liberal ideal, and a society which does not foster such diversity may well find its economic arteries hardening. While ebullient entrepreneurs do not by themselves make a good society, one that fails to provide opportunities for their enterprise to flourish will surely be poorer in more senses than the purely economic. For the provincial world, also, the preservation of independent centres of initiative which are not dominated by a metropolitan élite of central decision-makers in Whitehall and company head offices in London is an important objective which may be lost sight of. In Britain the danger of overcentralisation is particularly clear. Virtually all leading firms, many of which once had head offices in provincial centres, have now moved them to London. In the U.S., by contrast, only a proportion of corporations have head offices in New York: others are found in California, the Midwest and throughout the North Eastern States. One does not have to be an extremist liberal, believing that only the market and the competitive ethos can provide freedom and fulfilment, or a Celtic nationalist imagining that one's failures are the consequence of exploitation by the English, to recognise that highly centralised control of a society's resources has had formidable implications for the quality of political and social life in Britain. An analysis of industrial concentration which is concerned exclusively or even primarily with economic variables will therefore inevitably remain incomplete.

4 The Measurement of Concentration

We define the process of concentration as an increase in the extent to which economic activity is controlled by large firms. This definition requires expansion and explanation in at least four directions. First, what are the units in which economic activity is measured – sales, assets, employment or something else? Second, what is the area in which control is exercised – the industry, the region, the economy as a whole? Third, do we mean large in an absolute sense, or simply large relative to other firms in the same industry or economy? And fourth, once we have answered these questions and assembled our data, how do we combine them in a single summary measure of industrial structure – do we use concentration ratios, or one of the many other indices which have been proposed? None of these questions are of the kind to which there are right or wrong answers: there are particular ways of answering them which are more relevant for particular purposes, and, as we have argued in the preceding chapter, there are many different reasons for being interested in concentration. It is an empirical fact that it rarely matters how we answer them. The overall pattern of concentration and its trends are much the same however we choose to measure them. (Bates 1965, and pp. 93–7 below). The practically minded reader may therefore turn to the next chapter. He does, however, run some risk of being misled – though not, we add, by us. The necessary ambiguity about the concept of concentration has led some economists to use indicators which are, at best, only approximate measures. The man who wants to know whether or not to wear an overcoat and knows perfectly well what good weather means may quite reasonably dismiss discussion of whether it is more appropriately defined in terms of hours of sunshine or absence of cloud cover as mere meteorological pedantry. But he should know that some people interpret good weather as 'absence of rainfall': and while their descriptions are often accurate they can also be found in biting winds and sub-zero temperatures solemnly proclaiming that it is a nice day. The state of concentration measurement is much like that, and those who skip the more extensive argument below should at least consult our list of unreliable forecasters (p. 50 below.)

THE UNITS OF CONCENTRATION

There are many possible dimensions of economic power. Turnover (sales) is one, and for purposes of assessing market concentration it is the natural unit to take. For almost any other purpose, however, it is misleading, because firms vary so much in their degree of vertical integration. The *Times 1000*, published annually, ranks U.K. companies in order of their turnover. (A similar list is published for the U.S. by *Fortune* magazine.) In the top 20 in 1973–4, and ahead of Marks and Spencers and Allied Breweries, we find C. Czarnikow, a firm of commodity brokers employing around 300 people. It is difficult to argue that this is an accurate reflection of its role in the economic life of the U.K. Turnover systematically gives greater weight to distribution as against manufacture, and to assembly as against fully integrated processes. Assets and employment are in general more appealing. Both are relatively stable magnitudes, and the indications which they give are rarely counter-intuitive (unlike the case of Czarnikow's turnover). Since large firms tend to be more capital intensive than small, concentration will normally appear to be greater in terms of assets than in terms of employment. Employment would be the measure to choose if we were specifically interested in the impact of concentration on employees. A variant on this would be total payroll, relevant where we are not concerned solely with the number of workers but also with their qualitative contribution to the productive process, since full-time employees will receive more weight than part-time, and skilled more than unskilled. If we were interested in the economic power conferred by control of capital rather than labour, then assets might be more appropriate units.

But assets suffer from the deficiencies of the accounting data from which they are compiled: they represent a summation of the costs of items purchased at different prices and different dates, depreciated in accordance with arbitrary conventions. There are important omissions: leading retailers like Marks and Spencers report returns on capital of 30%–40%, not because they are wicked monopolists – there are numerous competitors, and many of them earn much lower rates of return – but because their principal asset, their accumulated good reputation and retailing expertise, is not reflected in their balance sheet. Yet it is an asset, acquired at some cost, depreciating in the absence of further investment, requiring maintenance expenditures, yielding a stream of returns into the future, no less real because intangible (Rees 1969). These factors are reflected in share prices, and it is possible to argue that the value the stock market attaches to a company is a better indicator of the true value of its assets than the figures which appear in its accounts. If the price of a share was always equal to the present value of the expected future profits of the company, this would be true: but, though there is some correspondence between the two, share prices are ultimately determined by the demand for and supply of particular kinds of risky assets. Quite apart from this, the use of this criterion would have some disturbing consequences. For example it would lead us to the conclusion that British Leyland Motors, as of 1974, was a concern of small significance. The stock market took the view that there was no prospect of its existing assets being operated profitably, and hence by implication that they were of negligible value: and we have little doubt that this judgement was correct. Nevertheless a concern with a very large collection of very unprofitable assets is not quite the same thing as a concern with no assets at all, and a measure which implies that is not the ideal for which we are looking.

Of course there is no such ideal, but the nearest approach to it may well be value added, the contribution of the enterprise to national income. It takes some account of both capital and labour employed, and it avoids obvious anomalies like those described above. Its overwhelming disadvantage is that as a rule we do not have any information about it. And this should bring us back to reality, and the realisation that the examples above are all extreme cases, chosen for illustrative purposes only; that in practice all these variables – sales, assets, employment, payroll, market capitalisation, value added – are likely to be closely correlated; and that the principal factor governing our choice is not these theoretical considerations but the availability of data. Studies of industrial concentration generally employ information derived from the census of production, and are based on sales or employment. These censuses normally divulge information on the share in sales and employment of the largest three, four or five firms, but they will not disclose information about individual companies. For our purpose of analysing contributions to concentration increase, however, it is essential to know this. We are therefore obliged to use measures which are available on a company by company basis – market value, obtainable from the financial press, and net assets, which are measured in company accounts. Since 1967 British companies have been obliged to reveal a much wider range of information on turnover, number of employees and total remuneration. We make some use of these figures – even trying to make a stab at value added – but the real beneficiaries will be those who write the equivalent of this book in fifty years' time.

THE DOMAIN OF CONCENTRATION

It is useful to distinguish market or industry concentration from aggregate concentration. Market concentration is concerned with particular products or product groups, and is the main focus of attention of those who are concerned with the exercise of monopoly power or some of the other narrower economic effects of concentration. There are many problems in defining industries for this purpose. First, it is clear that the more narrowly an industry is defined, the higher the degree of concentration is likely to be. The market for cars is more concentrated than that for vehicles, and that for Ford cars is more concentrated still. Both Britain and America have (different) industrial classifications, with three levels of definition: in the U.K., the order (food, drink and tobacco), the industry or minimum list heading (milk products), and the product group (ice cream). In the U.S. these are rather more memorably called two, three and four digit industries. The intention is that each level should represent the same degree of specialisation, and it is normal to compare the extent of concentration at the same level of definition: though there seems little reason to suppose that the intention has succeeded and that organic chemicals (product group) can reasonably be compared with fellmongery (product group) but not with milk products (industry).

Naming these headings makes clear that it is necessary to consider the principles on which to define product and industry groups. We can do this either by bringing together products which are good substitutes in consumption, or those which are good substitutes as far as producers are concerned. Fruit and cheese are both acceptable desserts, but they are generally provided by different organisations and it is not easy to switch productive capacity from one to the other. By contrast food mixers are poor alternatives to vacuum cleaners, but they are frequently made by the same firms from similar components. Each of these pairs is normally placed in the same industrial order, the industrial classification employing what is called a 'common-sense' approach. Nevertheless it seems clear that supply side considerations are normally dominant, so that washing machines are grouped with refrigerators, which are not very good at cleaning clothes, rather than with laundries, which are. This is hardly surprising, since the main purpose of industrial classification is to organise data on production, and a demand-biased system would lead to firms straddling several industries in an awkward manner. Nevertheless it means that the degree of industrial concentration appears to be much higher than it would be if a differently biased scheme were adopted, since the same firm frequently produces both members of the meaningless washing machine-refrigerator pair but not the meaningful laundry-washing machine pair. It also means that the tendency to increased industrial concentration over time is exaggerated, since firms are much more likely to diversify into fields with similar supply technologies than similar final uses: our washing machine manufacturer is much more likely to start making refrigerators than to set up a laundry. (Although the notion that the pursuit of monopoly power is a major cause of concentration increase might suggest the reverse.) These difficulties do not appear to have received proper attention, and commentators have been ready to accept whatever industrial classification is offered them more or less uncritically, although there is some discussion in the literature (e.g. by Evely and Little 1960) of the problems of specialisation (the extent to which a firm in a particular trade manufactures the products of other trades) and exclusiveness (the extent to which the product of a particular trade is made by firms allocated to other trades). If two product groups had identical market structures, the potential for monopoly power in them would only be the same if all the products within each group were equally good substitutes for each other, the pattern of cross-elasticities of demand between these and all other products were similar and similar relationships held on the supply side (reflecting equal ease of entry to and exit from the two industries). Merely to state these requirements is to indicate how impossibly far from fulfilment they are in any practical case.

The second major problem in defining the boundaries of the market is posed by the existence of foreign trade. Concentration ratios derived from the census of production normally relate to shares in domestic output. Thus exports are included, and, since large firms export a lower proportion of their output than small (see Table 2.1 above), we can expect that generally their share of domestic sales will be understated. But the main difficulty is not the inclusion of exports but the exclusion of imports. This could lead to ludicrous results: the lonely British banana grower, fighting a hopeless battle against impossible odds, would find that the price of being the only man foolish enough to enter the industry was to be branded a monopolist. And it would be facile to regard the increase in concentration in the U.K. between 1957 and 1969 as evidence of growing monopoly power without taking some explicit account of the fact that imports of manufactures grew sevenfold over the period. Clearly imports should be included in the denominator of any concentration ratio, though this is rarely done. An exception is Shepherd (1972) who showed that while U.K. industries were more concentrated than U.S. industries when shares in domestic output were considered, the positions were reversed when imports were brought into account. But this is not enough. Most economists and more businessmen would feel that a 20% market share for imports was a much more significant competitive force than a 20% market share held by small firms. The reason, we suspect, is that the rest of the world is capable of greatly increasing its market share with an ease which small firms cannot hope to emulate: the threat which it represents is correspondingly greater. And this should warn us that the difficulties of accounting for imports are merely the symptom of a more fundamental problem. Potential competition is almost as potent an influence on business behaviour as actual competition, but it is only the latter that we can hope to measure satisfactorily.

At this point the reader may wonder whether the measurement of market concentration is an exercise of any value at all. We sympathise, but feel that to abandon the attempt altogether would be to throw out the – admittedly rather small – baby with the – admittedly rather grubby – bathwater. The proper test of the relevance of an economic concept is its explanatory power, and the studies we have cited in the preceding chapter suggest that market concentration does have some, though we should hardly be surprised to find that it does not have much. We do think that there is more scope for the abuse of market power by the highly concentrated tobacco or spirits producers than in construction or in textiles, and that industrial economists comparing the degree of concentration in different markets are often saying something useful about industrial structures – though not always, and probably not as often as they imply. But we have no more confidence in the judgements of those who attach significance to movements of one or two percentage points in the concentration ratio than we have in examiners who claim to be able to distinguish a 59 % script from a 60 %. The economist assessing market concentration should be continuously alive to the possibilities and actualities of substitute commodities, foreign trade and new entry. He should be especially critical of policy recommendations based on the naïve and unqualified use of concentration indices without proper regard to the wider market context. American antitrust guidelines, effectively prohibiting firms with market shares above 25 % from acquiring competitors with more than 1 % of the market, are a good example of this. The British Monopolies Commission's restraint of Courtaulds' expansion into Lancashire textiles, on the basis of similar but predictably less clearly defined criteria, is another. Anyone who believes that the British textile industry is in danger of successful monopolisation cannot see beyond the Straits of Dover: he might care to go and talk to some redundant textile workers instead.

The discussion so far relates to market concentration. Our main interest in this volume is not in monopoly in particular industries, but in aggregate concentration, and so we need worry less about the depressing list of problems above. The appropriate domain of concentration for these purposes is the national economy, and for the purposes of this volume we narrow it further to the manufacturing sector (principally because of the problems of data availability and comparability which a wider coverage would raise.) Perhaps one day it will be appropriate to study aggregate concentration in a European context, but it is still some way off.

RELATIVE VERSUS ABSOLUTE MEASURES OF CONCENTRATION

In thinking about the economic role of large enterprises, we might mean large in some absolute sense, or we might mean large relative to all other enterprises. If all firms, large and small, grew by the same proportion, this absolute concept would indicate that concentration had gone up while the relative measure would show that it had remained the same. Which is more appropriate depends on the context. If we are concerned about alienation of workers, then what matters is that the plant they are working in has become bigger, and their reactions are not modified by the observation that the plant along the road has grown in size as well: an absolute measure is required. For other purposes, however, we may be interested in what has happened to the share of output held by large firms, and attach little importance to the fact that the output they are sharing is a growing one. This is clearly true, for example, in studying market concentration where a relative concept is appropriate.

We lay principal emphasis in this book on relative concentration because we suspect that is what most readers will be interested in, and where no qualifying adjective appears the word 'relative' is implicit. We do however describe below the possibility of obtaining measures of absolute concentration: indeed we suspect that part of the reason for its neglect has been the absence of appealing indicators of it, a situation which we attempt to remedy. We should also note that the terms 'relative' and 'absolute' measures have gained some currency in the literature in a rather different sense from the one in which we have used them here, but we regard this use as a misleading one. In this usage, due to Lintner and Butters (1950), the terms absolute and relative concentration are used for what we describe below, more accurately, as measures of concentration and measures of inequality.

FINDING AN INDEX

Our purpose in this section is to derive the measures of concentration which we employ in the empirical part of the present study. The strategy we adopt is as follows. We begin by reiterating our definition: that the process of concentration is an increase in the extent to which economic activity is controlled by large firms. We then explore some of the consequences of that definition. This enables us to construct a list of properties of concentration measures. Some of these properties we regard as essential. They are such basic implications of the definition that measures which do not have them are not measures of concentration, but of something else. This does not necessarily mean they are useless – the price of fish is an interesting magnitude, it is just not a measure of concentration. Other properties are merely desirable, on grounds of analytical convenience or aesthetic appeal. And some are merely possible properties: we may be interested to know our measures have them, but would not be distressed to find that they did not. The advantages of such a list are that it enables us to discriminate in a systematic manner between the many alternative measures of concentration which have been proposed, and to define a range of indices which encompass the inevitable remaining ambiguity about the meaning of concentration. In this section we look at relative concentration only. The analysis draws extensively on results obtained by Atkinson (1970) and Kolm (1969) in the measurement of income inequality.

The simplest and most widely used concentration measure is the concentration ratio, the share of output, assets, sales, employment or whatever (from now on we use 'market share' as a convenient shorthand) held by the largest N firms, where N is some number chosen by the investigator or more usually by the census of production authorities. We shall employ the common convention of writing CRN for the N firm concentration ratio. The deficiencies of this measure are obvious, and widely recognised. The choice of N is arbitrary, much information is wasted and dramatic shifts in industrial structure can occur to which the index will be wholly impervious. So long as they affect only members of the top N, or the rest of the industry, the CRN is unaffected by them.

However any change in structure will certainly affect *some* concentration ratio – if only the appropriate one had been chosen the effect would have been registered. This suggests we might consider all possible concentration ratios. The simplest way to do this is to draw a concentration curve (Figure 4.1): we plot N on the x-axis and CRN on the y-axis. If, as is shown in the diagram, every concentration ratio in industry A is lower than that in industry B, then the concentration curve for industry A will lie below that of industry B at all points. When this happens, it seems difficult to dispute that industry B is the more concentrated. Whether one thinks of the large firms in an industry as the leading one, three or seventeen, their total market share is greater. Thus we propose as a first requirement for a concentration index

    (i) if one concentration curve lies entirely above another, it represents a higher level of concentration.

Of course, this criterion will not always enable us to make a ranking. Frequently, concentration curves will intersect, as with B and C. In cases like these, property (i) sheds no light on which industry is the more concentrated.

Some fifty years ago Dalton (1920) enunciated what he called the 'principle of transfers' as a basis for the measurement of income inequality. If a man were to lose income to someone richer than himself, he argued, that represented an increase in the degree of inequality in income distribution. This seems highly plausible, and we suggest that a similar argument can be applied to the measurement of concentration in industry. If a large firm wins a customer from a smaller firm, we would wish to say that concentration has gone up. By analogy with Dalton's argument, we shall call this the sales transfer principle, and define our second property of plausible concentration measures

    (ii) the sales transfer principle must hold.

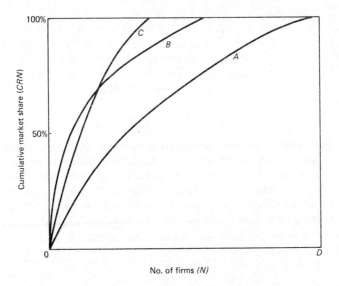

Fig. 4.1. Relative concentration curves

We must now think more generally about the effect on concentration of changes in industrial structure in the light of our basic definition that concentration is an increase in the economic role of large organisations. At first sight it might seem that the birth of a new firm is always a factor operating so as to reduce concentration. More careful consideration should lead us to modify this view: it is just possible that the new firm might gain such a large market share that we would feel that concentration had increased. The entry of the Xerox Corporation into the copying machine industry, for example, was hardly a force for deconcentration. But the entry of a small firm is certainly such a force, and we shall require that provided a new firm is not too large, its entry has the effect of reducing our concentration index. We shall consider more explicitly later how large we can allow it to be – we should certainly permit it to reach the average size of existing firms, for instance. Defining this property more rigorously, we have

(iii) there is some s, $0 < s < 1$, such that, if a new firm enters and gains market share $s_j \leq s$ while the relative shares of all existing firms are unchanged, concentration is reduced.

Conversely the exit of a firm (through bankruptcy for example) with size less than s increases the degree of concentration.

Entry and exit represent one type of discontinuous change in industrial structure: another is merger. When a merger or takeover occurs, one large firm replaces two smaller firms. Obviously this increases concentration. Hence we have our fourth property

(iv) merger increases concentration.

It is worth noting that properties (ii) and (iii) together imply property (iv). We can think of a merger in two stages – the transfer of all the sales of the smaller partner to the larger, followed by the exit from the industry of the now insignificant smaller firm. Since both these stages lead to concentration increases, so does the whole process.

UNSATISFACTORY MEASURES OF CONCENTRATION

This completes our list of essential properties of concentration measures. All of them follow as more or less immediate consequences of our definition. Although they impose quite mild restrictions, they nevertheless enable us to exclude a number of widely used measures. How does the concentration ratio, the commonest of all, stand up? Reasonably well, since although it does not necessarily react positively to a merger or sales transfer it will never be perverse in the direction of change. We can do better than this, but we can do quite a lot worse, and in Table 4.1 we provide a list of concentration measures which violate these axioms. The majority of these indices are defective because they measure inequality rather than concentration. To understand the distinction, imagine an economy dominated by a small number of giants of similar size. Now suppose many small firms enter, but enjoy little success, so that even in aggregate their market share is very low. Then concentration has not been significantly affected, but the degree of inequality in firms' sizes has greatly increased. We have little doubt that concentration is a much more interesting characteristic of industrial structure than the inequality of the size of firms. A similar distinction applies if we look at (for example) the distribution of income and wealth – the arrival of a boatload of

TABLE 4.1.   Unsatisfactory concentration indices

Measure	Definition	Axioms violated
variance	$\frac{1}{n}\Sigma s_i^2 - \frac{1}{n^2}(\Sigma s_i)^2$	(iii), (iv)
variance of logs	$\frac{1}{n}\Sigma(\log s_i)^2 - \frac{1}{n^2}(\Sigma \log s_i)^2$	all
slope of fitted Pareto curve	$(F(x) = Ax^{-b})$	all
Gini coefficient	$\frac{1}{n}(n+1-2\Sigma i s_i)$	(iii), (iv)
Hart's index (Hart 1971)	$\frac{1}{n}(n+1-\Sigma i s_i)$	(iii), (iv)
Hall–Tideman index (Hall and Tideman 1967)	$\dfrac{1}{2\Sigma i s_i - 1}$	(iii), (iv)
Redundancy	$\log n + \Sigma s_i \log s_i$	(iii), (iv)

(s_i is the share of the ith smallest firm; all summations are over all i)

impecunious immigrants leaves the concentration of wealth unchanged but increases the inequality. But the significance we attach to the measures is very different in this case. We are quite properly interested in both the concentration of wealth and the inequality of its distribution. We need measures of inequality here because we are concerned about individuals with no incomes. We are not much interested in firms with no sales.

We would not wish to exclude the possibility that there are some economic contexts in which the extent of inequality in the sizes of firms is an interesting variable, though we find ourselves unable to think of what they might be. Confusion has arisen because, if the number of firms remains constant, increases in inequality will be associated with increases in concentration. But of course the number of firms never does remain constant – entry, exit and amalgamation see to that, and in practice the two indicators will quite frequently move in opposite directions. Indeed it is very difficult to define the number of firms. Is the housewife who grinds her own salt, or the pharmacist who makes up some of his own medicines, a 'firm' in the chemical industry? Because inequality measures are very sensitive to the number of small firms, such decisions are of great importance, and will affect them quite as much as large changes in the sales of I.C.I. or Du Pont. It is puzzling that the many authors who have made use of inequality indices have devoted little or no space to these questions. For ourselves, we cannot believe that such semantic problems have any practical significance, and this seems to us to cast serious doubt on the utility of such indicators. But we are open to persuasion on this point, and merely wish to emphasise here that inequality and concentration are not the same thing: that trends in one do not necessarily shed light on trends in the other: and that our concern in this volume is with concentration.

It is tedious to labour what we hope the reader will find an obvious point. Our only justification for doing so is that the arguments above were laid out with great clarity and lucidity by Adelman (1951) all of twenty-five years ago, and that nevertheless economists have regularly continued to make unwarranted inferences about changes in concentration on the basis of measurements of inequality. We therefore conclude this discussion by looking more specifically at some properties of one measure in Table 4.1, the variance of logarithms, a measure used in some earlier studies of the principal subject of the present work. Consider an industry with three firms, with sales 1000, 100 and 1 respectively. The largest firm gains a customer from its closest competitor, so that sales are now 1001, 99 and 1. We cannot imagine that anyone would doubt that concentration has increased, but the variance of logarithms falls. More perversely still, if we had omitted the smallest of the firms (and given its relative insignificance it seems very likely that we would), the change would have been in the opposite direction. These deficiencies are not confined to artificially constructed examples involving small numbers of firms. In our empirical work we compared the actual 1919 distribution of firm sizes in the food industry with a hypothetical distribution incorporating the effects of all mergers occurring in the following twelve years. 58 of the 103 firms in the industry disappear through merger, and the largest firm, Unilever, acquires 19 of them, including seven of its fifteen largest competitors, and raises its market share from 22 % to 49 %. The CR5 rises from 39 % to 68 %, and the CR20 from 72 % to 94 %. A clearer case of concentration increase is hard to imagine, but the variance of logs records the process as a modest decline. The reason is the same as in our previous simple example; the logarithmic transformation greatly understates the significance of gains in sales by the largest firm. We can place no reliance on an indicator with these errant properties.

FURTHER PROPERTIES OF CONCENTRATION INDICES

The properties discussed above are intrinsic to the concept of concentration. We now go on to discuss a rather wider list of characteristics. These are of a somewhat different nature, and we would certainly not wish to argue that measures which do not fulfil them can necessarily be rejected. We develop them in order to obtain rather clearer insight into the nature of concentration, and to provide some basis for choice between alternatives. Our fifth property is rather strangely formulated. Imagine a model of firms' behaviour, in which the overall size of the market is static, but customers' allegiance to particular firms changes from time to time, so that the market share of individual businesses is variable. Specifically let us suppose that in any period the proportion of firm i's customers who defect to firm j is the same as the fraction of j's customers who transfer to i. This is a simple characterisation of a situation in which there is no evident relationship between present size and future success: rather similar in spirit to the Gibrat model, in which all firms expect to end the period with the same market share that they had at the beginning, although some in the end do rather better and others worse. However, its impact on concentration is exactly the opposite. If shoppers are equally likely to shift their business from Woolworths to the corner shop or from the corner shop to Woolworths, it is clear that in the long run the corner shop will win rather more new customers than Woolworths. So we designate this process the anti-Gibrat effect and define a fifth property

  (v) the 'anti-Gibrat' effect reduces concentration. This is similar to (though perhaps more compelling than) the concept of 'averages preference' discussed in Kolm (1969). Strictly we have in mind a rather weaker version of this anti-Gibrat effect than that described above. Let a_{ij} be the proportion of firm i's customers who transfer to firm j. Then we require only that $\sum_j a_{ij} = \sum_j a_{ji}$, for all i.

We noted above the difficulty of deciding exactly how many small firms there were, and the problems posed by the use of an indicator which was sensitive to such decisions. We shall rule out indices of this kind by invoking the following requirement

    (vi) let s_j be the market share of a new entrant. Then, as s_j tends to zero, so does its effect on a concentration index.

We can now disclose our reasons for introducing property (v) at this stage by stating the following theorem. *Properties (ii) (the sales transfer principle), (i) (the concentration curve ranking criterion) and (vi), and property (v) are equivalent, and each implies that an index should be a strictly S-convex function of the shares of individual firms.* (A function is strictly S-convex if $f(x) > f(Qx)$ for all bistochastic matrices Q and vectors x. A matrix Q is bistochastic if all elements are non-negative and all rows and columns sum to one.) It is not too difficult to gain an intuitive grasp of the equivalence: one or two experiments should persuade the reader that a sales transfer generates an upward shift in the concentration curve, and that the anti-Gibrat effect implies a sequence of transfers from large firms to small, (although the reverse implications are less obvious). For a formal proof, and for a demonstration that they imply the mathematical property of S-convexity, we use a theorem of Hardy, Littlewood and Polya (1934) in the form given by Dasgupta, Sen and Starrett (1973).

This states that for two vectors x and y in R^n ordered so that $x_1 \geq \ldots \geq x_n$ and $y_1 \geq \ldots \geq y_n$, then the following conditions are equivalent

    (a) there is a bistochastic matrix Q (not a permutation matrix) such that $y = Qx$.

    (b) $y_1 + \ldots + y_k \leq x_1 + \ldots + x_k$ for all $k \leq n$, with strict inequality for at least one k, and equality for $k = n$.

    (c) x can be obtained from y by a non empty finite series of transfers of the form

$$x'_r = x_r + e \qquad x'_{r+m} = x_{r+m} - e$$
$$x'_j = x_j \qquad j \neq r, r+m$$

    (d) $F(x) > F(y)$ for all strictly S-convex F.

Condition (a) represents a precise statement of our anti-Gibrat effect, while (b) is simply a statement for industries with equal numbers of firms of the condition that the concentration curves do not intersect. Since our condition (vi) implies that we can add or subtract sufficient zero-sized firms to obtain this equality without altering the ranking, (b) is equivalent to (i) and (vi); (c) describes a sequence of sales transfers, and hence our theorem follows.

All the properties discussed so far are ordinal rather than cardinal properties of concentration measures. They indicate whether an index should rise or fall in specified situations, but give us no clue as to how much it should rise or fall. For empirical work, and especially for the purpose of estimating the contribution of various elements to the growth of concentration, it is necessary for us to have a cardinal measure – to specify, in effect, the units in which concentration is to be measured. As a first step towards cardinalisation we can introduce a further property

  (vii) the Gibrat effect increases the expected value of the concentration index.

This will be true if the measure F introduced above is a strictly convex function of the vector of firm's shares $\{x\}$: if y_1 is a random variable with mean x_i, then $E\{F(y)\} > F(x)$ for all strictly convex F by immediate application of the definition of convexity. We can confirm that any function which is strictly convex and symmetric is strictly S-convex: by a theorem of Birkhoff and von Neumann (Berge 1963) any bistochastic matrix

$$Q = \lambda_1 P_1 + \lambda_2 P_2 + \ldots \lambda_n P_n$$

for some numbers $\lambda_1 \ldots \lambda_n$ and permutation matrices $P_1 \ldots P_n$. with $\lambda_1 + \lambda_2 + \ldots + \lambda_n = 1$.
Thus $Qx = \lambda_1 x_1 + \lambda_2 x_2 + \ldots + \lambda_n x_n$

where $x_1 \ldots x_n$ are permutations of the vector x.
Hence for any symmetric strictly convex function F, $F(Qx) > F(x)$ for any bistochastic Q: and so F is S-convex.

However there are many functions which meet these requirements. We still need to find a basis for choosing the unit of measurement of concentration. Two possibilities have been suggested. We are much attracted by the argument of Adelman (1969) that the most natural and intuitively persuasive unit of concentration is the equivalent number of equal sized firms. If asked 'how extensive is the degree of industrial concentration', one would like to reply by saying something like 'there are now about five hundred firms'. But we would be reluctant to do this, because we would immediately feel obliged to launch into a series of qualifications, explaining that the concept of a firm was actually rather blurred, that some of these firms were very large but most of them were very small, and so on. But if we could say 'it is rather as if there were three hundred firms of roughly equal size', we could give an answer which would not be misleading in these ways, and one which would be in terms which would be meaningful to the listener and enable him to make some assessment of his own of whether the degree of concentration was high or low. This intuitive significance is the principal advantage of the concentration ratio: but the numbers equivalent has it in even greater degree. (This point will probably be less obvious to economists, to whom the CR measure is familiar, than to the general reader.) Of course, there will be room for substantial and legitimate disagreement about the means by which the available data on industrial structure should be translated into a numbers equivalent, but that, we suggest, is a rather different question, and one to be decided in the light of the other properties discussed in this chapter. To be precise our requirement is that

F should have the property $F\left(\dfrac{1}{n}, \dfrac{1}{n} \ldots \dfrac{1}{n}\right) = n$. The use of numbers

equivalent as unit does have the minor disadvantage that it goes up when concentration goes down and vice versa, but this is unlikely to be found a serious problem.

Another basis for cardinalisation has been suggested by Hall and Tideman (1967). They argue that if all firms in an industry were split into k bits, the concentration index should be reduced by a

proportion $\left(\dfrac{1}{k}\right)$. We believe it would be in the spirit of their proposal to

agree that it would also be acceptable for the measure to be multiplied by k, where (as with the numbers equivalent) it is an inverse function of the degree of concentration. We do not find this argument as compelling as Adelman's, but do consider that it has some appeal.

A PROPOSED RANGE OF MEASURES

We have argued that an index of concentration might have the following properties
  – that it should concur with the ranking of the concentration curves
  – that it should fulfil the sales transfer principle
  – that merger implies increased concentration
  – that the Gibrat effect increases concentration
  – and that the anti-Gibrat effect reduces it
  – that it should not be affected significantly by the entry or exit of insignificant firms.

The indices we propose to use in this study are the simplest kind of symmetric convex functions. They are additively separable, and have the form Σs_i^α where s_i is the share of firm i. We translate into a numbers equivalent: n firms each with share $\dfrac{1}{n}$ would register a value $n^{1-\alpha}$ so that our index has the form

$$n(\alpha) = \left(\sum_i s_i^\alpha\right)^{\frac{1}{1-\alpha}} \qquad \alpha > 0 \qquad \alpha \neq 1$$

As symmetric convex functions they possess all the properties outlined above, and they also meet the Adelman and Hall-Tideman cardinalisation criteria. α is a parameter capable of variation to reflect alternative views of concentration which might be held by political scientists, sociologists or economists. We have argued that a certain amount of ambiguity is intrinsic to the concentration concept. What we are seeking to do in proposing this set of measures is to retain sufficient generality for the inevitable ambiguity to be reflected in the different behaviour of different elements, while restricting the degree of generality sufficiently to make the analysis manageable. The extent to which we have succeeded in this aim is an empirical question, and the reader must make his own judgement on the basis of what follows.

The role of the elasticity parameter α is to enable us to decide how much weight to attach to the upper portion of the distribution relative to the lower. This can be seen most easily by considering limiting cases. As $\alpha \to 0$, the index simply approaches the number of firms: as $\alpha \to \infty$, it tends towards the reciprocal of the share of the largest firm. In general, high α gives greater weight to the role of the largest firms in the distribution: lower α emphasises the presence or absence of small firms. As an example, consider two industries. In one, there are only two firms, and output is equally divided between them. In another, the largest firm has 70% of the market, and three small firms have 10% each. Which industry is more concentrated? Clearly two views are possible. Some economists might feel that the complete absence of small firms in the first industry implied that the level of concentration was higher there, while others might think the overwhelming importance of one giant firm in the second was decisive. Our elasticity parameter reflects this divergence. If α is less than 1·8, the duopoly appears more concentrated: above that value, the ranking is reversed.

We should draw attention to two special cases of our measure. If α takes the value 2, then our index is simply the familiar and widely used Herfindahl index, attributed to Herfindahl (1950) and Hirschman (1964) and popularised by Stigler (1968), presented in the numbers equivalent form as proposed by Adelman (1969). The discussion of the economic theory of oligopoly in Chapter 2 lends some theoretical support to this measure. If $\alpha = 1$, then $n(\alpha)$ is undefined: however we may look at the limit of n as $\alpha \to 1$. Let $\alpha = 1 + h$. Then as $h \to 0$, $s_i^\alpha \to s_i + h s_i \log s_i$, by Taylor expansion of s_i^α, and hence $\sum_i s_i^\alpha \to 1 + h \sum_i s_i \log s_i$.

Thus $\log \sum_i s_i^\alpha \to h \sum_i s_i \log s_i$. From the definition of $n(\alpha)$,

$$\log n(\alpha) = \frac{1}{1-\alpha} \log \sum_i s_i = -\frac{1}{h} \log \sum_i s_i.$$

Hence as $\alpha \to 1$, $\lim \log n(\alpha) = -\sum_i s_i \log s_i$. Now $\sum_i s_i \log s_i$ is the Theil

(1967) entropy index of concentration, so that the argument shows that for α sufficiently close to 1 the ranking given by our index will be the same as that given by entropy. The limit of n as $\alpha \to 1$ is therefore exp $-\sum_i s_i \log s_i$, and that is the value which we report for $\alpha = 1$ in our subsequent work. Some theoretical justification for the use of this figure in sociological contexts is provided in Chapter 3 above.

In completing our theoretical discussion of the properties of these measures, we should return to an issue raised earlier: what is the effect of new entry on the concentration index? Suppose the existing firms have sizes $\{a_i\}$, making the total size of the industry A. Thus the initial value of the index is $n = \left\{ \sum \left(\dfrac{a_i}{A} \right)^\alpha \right\}^{\frac{1}{1-\alpha}}$. Corresponding to n, the number of equivalent equal sized firms, we have $\dfrac{1}{n}$, the market share which a firm of this size would have, which we can regard as the effective average share of all firms. As $\dfrac{1}{n}$ is the effective average share, $\dfrac{A}{n}$ is the effective average size of the firms. Now suppose a new firm of size a enters the industry. Then the new value of our index is n' and the increase in it is

$$n' - n = \left\{ \left(\frac{a}{A+a} \right)^\alpha + \sum \left(\frac{a_i}{A+a} \right)^\alpha \right\}^{\frac{1}{1-\alpha}} - \left\{ \sum \left(\frac{a_i}{A} \right)^\alpha \right\}^{\frac{1}{1-\alpha}} \frac{\partial(n'-n)}{\partial a}$$

$$= \frac{\alpha}{1-\alpha} \left\{ \left(\frac{a}{A+a} \right)^\alpha + \sum \left(\frac{a_i}{A+a} \right)^\alpha \right\}^{\frac{\alpha}{1-\alpha}} \times$$

$$\left\{ \left(\frac{a}{A+a} \right)^{\alpha-1} \cdot \frac{A}{(A+a)^2} - \left(\frac{1}{A+a} \right)^{\alpha+1} \sum a_i^\alpha \right\}$$

It can easily be checked that as $a \to 0$, $n' \to n$, and that at $a = 0$ $\dfrac{\partial(n'-n)}{\partial a} > 0$. so that insignificant new entry has insignificant impact on concentration, but nevertheless reduces it. How large does a new entrant have to be for its deconcentrating effect to be at a maximum? Set $\dfrac{\partial(n'-n)}{\partial a}$ equal to zero, and we find that $\dfrac{a}{A} = \left\{ \sum \left(\dfrac{a_i}{A} \right)^\alpha \right\}^{-\frac{1}{1-\alpha}} = \dfrac{1}{n}$. Substitute for a, and we have $n' - n = 1$. In other words new entry will be most powerful in reducing concentration if the newcomer's size is equal to the effective average size of the existing firms, and it will in that case increase the numbers equivalent measure by one. If the new firm is larger, then its effect in reducing the share of the existing large firms is offset to some extent by the fact that it is a large firm itself. If the new firm were sufficiently large, it is conceivable (though unlikely) that this second factor might outweigh the first. A related question is the effect which the growth of an existing firm has on concentration. If the firm is sufficiently small, we would want concentration to decline: if it is one of the larger firms in the industry, it would rise. What is the critical size at which growth can occur without altering concentration? The preceding argument suggests 'the effective average', and analysis confirms this. We have $n = \left\{ \sum \left(\dfrac{a_i}{A} \right)^\alpha \right\}^{\frac{1}{1-\alpha}}$.

Differentiating gives $\dfrac{\partial n}{\partial a_j} = \dfrac{\alpha}{1-\alpha} \left\{ \dfrac{a_j^{\alpha-1}}{A^\alpha} n^{\frac{\alpha}{1-\alpha}} - \dfrac{1}{A} n^{\frac{1}{1-\alpha}} \right\}$. Setting $\dfrac{\partial n}{\partial a_j} = 0$ shows $a_j = \dfrac{1}{n}$. Both these properties confirm the generally attractive characteristics of our measures.

AN INDEX OF ABSOLUTE CONCENTRATION

As noted, the discussion above relates entirely to relative concentration. We now consider, more briefly, the choice of an index of absolute concentration. Such a measure will be a function, not of the relative shares of individual firms, but of their actual sizes, measured in terms of whatever unit of size – assets, employment, etc. – we have chosen. We could list essential and desirable properties of such a measure in much the same way as we have done for relative concentration. Some of the properties would apply here also without qualifications: the sales transfer principle – that a gain in sales by a large firm at the expense of a small should increase concentration – is equally applicable. Others would need some modification. Our concentration curve would now appear as in Figure 4.2; it would show, not the share of the largest n firms, but the actual volume of assets they controlled. The concentration curve would give an unambiguous ranking only if the largest N firms controlled a smaller quantity of assets in one industry than in another for all values of N. This will be true only if, *inter alia*, the potentially less concentrated industry is (measured by the total volume of its assets) smaller. Again the list of fundamental characteristics will enable us to impose mild restrictions on the class of acceptable measures: they will have to be S-convex functions of the sizes of the individual firms. Instead of elaborating this analysis, which would be on very similar lines to those covered in preceding sections, we move directly to its conclusions. We have shown how any particular industrial structure can be translated into an equivalent number of equal sized firms. Our measure of relative concentration will be the number of such firms: our measure of absolute concentration will be the size of such a firm. It will be derived simply by dividing the total of assets, or whatever units are chosen, by n. It is therefore the effective average size of a firm and we measure absolute

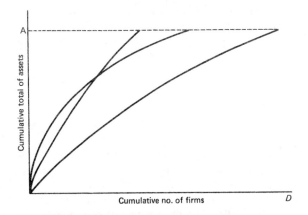

Fig. 4.2. Absolute concentration curves

concentration in the same dimensions as those in which we measure the size of a firm. We say 'effective average', because this figure is a weighted average; without such weighting, it would be unduly influenced by the number of small firms, since the formation of I.C.I. could be offset by the simultaneous formation of a modest number of one man businesses.

This indicator will be defined as

$$M(\alpha) = \frac{A}{n} = A \left\{ \sum \left(\frac{a_i}{A} \right)^{\alpha} \right\}^{\frac{1}{\alpha - 1}}$$

In this context the two properties defined at the end of the preceding section seem especially persuasive. We have defined an 'equivalent average size' of firm which rises if a larger firm enters, and falls if a newcomer is smaller. It goes up if growth occurs in a bigger firm, down if it happens in one that is smaller. The search for a measure of this kind was inaugurated by Niehans (1958), and the index he proposed was $\sum \left(\frac{a_i^2}{A} \right)$. This is equivalent to the special case of our measure where $\alpha = 2$. Thus the Niehans index is simply the absolute concentration measure corresponding to Herfindahl's concentration index.

THE MEASURES IN PRACTICE

We now resume our discussion of relative concentration. The preceding argument has enabled us to reject a number of deficient concentration indicators, and to construct a range of measures with what we believe are attractive properties. However the range with different elasticity parameters (α) is by no means the only possible set of measures which fulfil what we have regarded as the essential properties of concentration measures. The principal unresolved question is whether the range we have proposed is sufficiently wide to include all reasonable views of the determinants of concentration. Is it possible that there might be legitimate disagreement about which of two industries was more concentrated, even though all our measures pointed in one direction? This is an empirical question, and one which we tackle in two ways. First, we describe the tests we have conducted which persuade us that, where real ambiguity exists, our indicators reflect it. In these cases, one industry is more concentrated for some values of α but not others. Second, we present in the following section an opportunity for the reader to assess for himself the kind of situation in which our measures give equivocal results, and to see to what extent these uncertainties mirror his own.

Our trials were conducted on a range of real populations of firms, which generated a total of 256 pairwise comparisons. In 155 of these cases the concentration curves did not intersect, so that the rankings obtained were unambiguous. Of the remaining 101, a substantial number of intersections appeared to us to be trivial. The most common case of this kind arose when a population, which intuition suggested was more concentrated, had a fairly large number of very small firms in it. In such a case, the ambiguity would disappear if one removed from the population a group of firms whose combined share was two or three per cent of the market. To believe that this should significantly affect the ranking is to attach great weight to the mere existence of firms. There are also some trivial intersections at the top of the distribution. These occur where one population appears clearly less concentrated than another – except that the top firm is slightly larger. Of course, if the difference is substantial, there is genuine ambiguity about the ranking of the two populations. But where the difference is slight and the leading firm not exceptionally large, it would involve a very exaggerated view of the importance of the top firm to consider that this factor should exert decisive influence on the comparison.

For α sufficiently high or low, our index will reflect such 'trivial' ambiguities. But we think it inappropriate that it should do so: we want indicators which take proper account of the whole distribution, and do not reflect simply the size of the largest firm or the number of firms in the population. For the primary purpose for which we use our measure – evaluating the significance of merger – we believe such extreme indicators are of little interest. We therefore truncated the range of values of α used in our study. The range we employed was $\alpha = 0.6$ to $\alpha = 2.5$. This choice was based on inspection of direct pair-wise comparisons of 'transitions': cases where two different size distributions are ranked differently by different values of α. We felt that in the cases where the transition, at which the two distributions were rated equally, occurred outside this particular range, there was little room for reasonable doubt as to which of the two distributions was more concentrated. The reader can make his own assessment of the validity of this viewpoint, and can decide which value of α best reflects his own intuitive perception of the determinants of concentration, by considering the transitions cited below. Thirty eight of the 101 intersections were trivial on the basis of this criterion.

Where concentration curves intersect only once (or an odd number of times), there is certainly some α which ranks the two curves equally. For an even number of intersections, this will not necessarily be true. Our 256 comparisons yielded ten cases of multiple intersections. In five of these cases, we felt confident in saying that one of the two populations was more concentrated. In two cases there were transitions for some values of α within our range.

This left three of the 256 cases which we regarded as failures. These were cases of multiple intersection of concentration curves, where it seemed to us there was room for reasonable argument about which distribution was more concentrated, but where our index gave an unequivocal result. However this is a sufficiently low failure rate for us to feel reasonably reassured by the results of these comparisons. The class of concentration indices we have employed is a restricted one. Nevertheless we believe that most of the ambiguity about the 'true' meaning of concentration is reflected within that restricted class of indices.

APPENDIX

Calibrate your own concentration index
In this appendix we consider more empirically the nature of the difficulties involved in reaching a single measure of concentration by illustrating a number of cases in our work in which the concentration curves failed to give an unambiguous ranking. In each example the ten individual figures cited are the percentage shares of the ten largest firms, and the number in brackets which follows is their total share – the CR10.

Comparison 1
Industry 1   9·3 5·8 4·6 4·6 4·4 3·9 3·5 2·8 2·7 2·6 (44·3)
              The top 50 firms have 84% of the market.
              The remaining 16% is shared by 88 firms.
Industry 2   25·4 9·0 5·6 3·8 3·6 3·4 2·8 2·5 2·5 2·0 (60·7)
              The top 50 firms have 84% of the market.
              The remaining 16% is shared by 165 firms.
In this comparison we imagine that almost everyone would agree that the second industry was the more highly concentrated. The share of the top firm is much larger: and, even if it were ignored, the next ten firms have

about half the remaining market, which is significantly higher than the CR10 for industry 1. Indeed for all values of the CRN down to the CR50, industry 2 appears as the more highly concentrated. The only cause for doubt is that the tail of very small firms is much larger in industry 2 than it is in 1. This is not a trivial effect either, but a significant characteristic of the industries (which are respectively metal manufacture and textiles); there is much more scope for small-scale enterprise in textiles than in steel manufacture or in aluminium smelting. Nevertheless the quantitative significance even of all these small firms taken together is not very great. These two industries are ranked equally at $\alpha = 0.65$, close to the boundaries of the range of values of α we have considered reasonable. Above 0.65 textiles appears as more highly concentrated: below 0.65 metal manufacture is more concentrated.

Comparison 2

Industry 1   13·0 10·5 9·3 8·1 5·4 4·6 4·1 2·3 2·2 2·2 (61·7)
               The top 20 firms have 77% of the market.
               The remaining 23% is shared by 50 firms.
Industry 2   22·0 5·8 3·9 3·9 3·3 3·2 2·8 2·8 2·7 2·6 (52·8)
               The top 20 firms have 72% of the market.
               The remaining 28% is shared by 83 firms.

Comparison 2, we suspect, will cause most people more difficulty. In industry 2 there is a dominant firm, with a market share of almost a quarter. In 1 there are several large firms of roughly equal size. The role of the relatively small firms in the competitive fringe is clearly much greater in 2 than in 1. There is considerable room here for reasonable men to disagree about the relative extent of concentration in the two industries. This 'transition' falls right in the centre of our range. For $\alpha < 1.27$, industry 1 is the more highly concentrated; for $\alpha > 1.27$, industry 2 is ranked on top.

Now consider Comparison 3 below. On most criteria we would judge that 1 was the more concentrated industry. There are few small firms, and the industry is overwhelmingly dominated by the giants. For all values of the CRN beyond 1, the second industry appears less concentrated. The only qualification to this view is that in 2 the share of the largest firm is significantly greater. It would require very great emphasis on this fact to create serious doubt as to the order in which these industries should be ranked. A transition occurs here at $\alpha = 2.4$, right at the top of our range of relevant values of α. For all α below this, the first industry is the more highly concentrated.

Comparison 3

Industry 1   19·8 17·2 9·2 8·6 6·5 5·3 4·7 2·1 1·8 1·6 (76·7)
               The top 20 firms have 85% of the market; the top 50: 96%.
               The rest is shared by 43 firms.

Industry 2 25·4 9·0 5·6 3·8 3·6 3·4 2·8 2·5 2·5 2·0 (60·7)

> The top 20 firms have 70 % of the market, and the largest 50 have 84 %; the rest is shared by 165 firms.

We hope that these comparisons will give the reader some greater confidence in the views which we have formed after the rather more extensive trials of this kind reported above:

(i) that there can be a good deal of doubt about levels of concentration where ambiguity occurs in the range $\alpha = 1$ to $\alpha = 2$, and the presentation of a range of values is useful in such cases.

(ii) that $\alpha = 0.6$ and $\alpha = 2.5$ represent extreme ends of the range of interesting values.

5 The Historical Trend –
1919–57

It was not until the Second World War that economists began to measure market structures in Britain. For many years the partial nature of the data – and the lack of a clear understanding of the characteristics of appropriate measures – left a good deal of room for disagreement about the magnitude and direction of the long-run trend in concentration. Despite the fairly obvious facts that Victorian industry had been characterised by many small competing firms and that the modern economy was dominated by large ones, the available statistical studies were so imperfect that it was possible (though not very plausible) to argue that the first half of the century had seen little increase in concentration levels (e.g. Hunter 1969). More recently, as we have seen from Figure 1.1, the picture has become clearer. There is still room for disagreement about trends over the short term, but there is no doubt that the share of the largest 100 firms is substantially higher now than it was at the turn of the century. Before the 1960s the most conspicious period of rapidly rising concentration in the twentieth century was the 1920s, and we chose this for our pilot investigation using our suggested range of concentration measures.

In this period neither Census of Production information nor company accounting data are available in a form suitable for the analysis of concentration. It was therefore necessary to adopt as a measure of size the market valuation of companies and this obliged us to confine our study to that upper tail of firms in manufacturing industry for which some estimate of asset value could be made from stock exchange data. The construction of such estimates for January 1919 and December 1930 is described more fully in the appendix. The resulting population includes all London quoted companies and a variety of other sizeable companies, though it omits many small (and a few large) unquoted companies. Those which are omitted are, however, omitted both in 1919 and 1930 (unless they were genuinely founded or liquidated during the period), so that in this sense our population is a constant one. This does not, however, guarantee that the proportion of manufacturing industry covered by our sample is stable as between 1919 and 1930, for the position of the constant number of firms in our sample may be changing relative to the position of the smaller, excluded firms. Between 1919 and

1930 the total market values of our population rose by 54%, whereas over the same period share prices rose by only 15% (Moodies 1976) and the capital stock by only 6% (Feinstein 1972): it is likely that some of this discrepancy reflects gains by our population at the expense of smaller firms and hence that any rise in concentration will be understated. It is difficult to assess precisely the proportion of total manufacturing output accounted for by our population but, on the basis of a benchmark estimate of the share of large firms in total profits (Hannah 1972, p. 203), we would guess that our population accounted for between 40% and 50% of manufacturing profits. It is therefore a sufficiently broad sample of manufacturing industry to be of some interest in its own right, and it is not implausible that trends in concentration within this population will reflect general changes in manufacturing industry.

TABLE 5.1. Concentration in U.K. manufacturing industry 1919–30

1	*2*	*3*	*4*	*5*
Measure	1919	Change due to merger	Change due to internal growth	1930
CRN (per cent)				
$N = 50$	43·4	+ 13·9	+ 6·4	= 63·7
$N = 100$	56·4	+ 16·1	+ 4·9	= 77·4
$N = 200$	70·1	+ 16·3	+ 3·0	= 89·4
$N = 500$	88·0	+ 11·1	+ 0·5	= 99·6
Numbers equivalent				
$\alpha = 0$	1263	− 671	− 8	= 584
$\alpha = 0·6$	645	− 350	− 48	= 247
$\alpha = 0·8$	506	− 274	− 50	= 182
$\alpha = 1·0$	395	− 212	− 48	= 135
$\alpha = 1·2$	312	− 167	− 44	= 101
$\alpha = 1·4$	249	− 131	− 40	= 78
$\alpha = 1·6$	203	− 105	− 35	= 63
$\alpha = 1·8$	169	− 86	− 31	= 52
$\alpha = 2·0$	144	− 73	− 27	= 44
$\alpha = 2·5$	104	− 50	− 21	= 33

Table 5.1 presents a range of alternative measures of concentration within our population for 1919 (Col. 2) and 1930 (Col. 5). It is evident from the familiar concentration ratios that concentration was indeed increasing rapidly: the CR100, for example, increases from 56·4% to 77·4% over the twelve-year period. Similar increases occur for all the CRNs presented. We also present in Table 5.1 the measures of concentration suggested by our theoretical discussion in Chapter 4,

incorporating the variable elasticity parameter α. In its numbers equivalent form this index falls when concentration rises: logically, a more concentrated industry is one with fewer 'equivalent equally-sized firms'. As we should expect – since the direction of the change shown by different CRNs is quite unequivocal – a rise in concentration is shown for all values of α. At $\alpha = 0$ our index is simply the number of firms which declines from 1263 to 584. At $\alpha = 1$ (equivalent to the entropy concentration index), the change in concentration may be characterised as a reduction in the number of 'equivalent firms' from 395 to 135; at $\alpha = 2$, which gives more weight to the larger firms (and is equivalent to the Herfindahl index), there is a reduction in the number of 'equivalent firms' from 144 to 44. Thus the change in concentration is broadly equivalent in its effect on market structure to that of two-thirds of all firms being eliminated from the manufacturing sector. It is therefore a spectacularly large increase.

Table 5.1 also shows the sources of this rise in concentration, distinguishing between internal growth and merger. In order to determine their relative contribution, we constructed a hypothetical population of firms which reflects what the population would have looked like in 1919 if all the mergers of 1919–30 had occurred in that year. We were able to identify the relevant mergers from reports in business histories and the financial press and from a listing of the firms which disappeared from our population between 1919 and 1930 (almost all firm disappearances in our population of relatively large firms were a result of merger). On the basis of this information we 'merged' the firms of 1919 with their prospective partners of the next twelve years. By comparing this hypothetical population with the actual distribution we obtain an estimate of the contribution of mergers to rising concentration (Col. 3); the residual growth in concentration by 1930 can be attributed to the internal growth of firms (Col. 4).

(In interpreting the relative importance of internal growth and merger, attention should be focused on the proportionate reduction in the number of equivalent firms at each stage. Thus at $\alpha = 1\cdot6$, the number of 'equivalent firms' is reduced by about half ($105 \div 203$) by merger, and by a further third ($35 \div (203 - 105)$) by internal growth.)

For all values of α and all reported CRNs, mergers are clearly the main force behind rising concentration, accounting for more than half of the recorded rise. Moreover it is clear that these are lower bound estimates of the importance of merger, for, although we have included all major mergers, such as the formation of I.C.I. and Unilever, there were many smaller and medium-sized mergers in this period which because of data limitations we were obliged to exclude (Hannah 1976, appendix 1). *Faute de mieux* some such mergers appear in our table as contributing to internal growth.

Our estimate of the importance of merger rests on the counterfactual hypothesis that, in the absence of merger, the independent firms would have proportionately maintained the same market shares as the merged company. Plausible arguments might be constructed to suggest that this will result in an overestimate or an underestimate of the impact of merger: if the merger resulted in the achievement of economies of scale, then its growth would have been greater than the independent companies would have achieved; while, if it ran into serious management problems, the opposite would be the case. However a more precise estimate of the counterfactual population which would have existed in the absence of merger would clearly pose insurmountable research problems, and we are fully persuaded by the arguments advanced in the American context (Stigler 1956, *contra* Weston 1953) that the assumption implicit in our counterfactual population is superior to the alternative assumption that the effect of an acquisition is appropriately measured by its absolute size at the time of acquisition, irrespective of later joint growth or decline.

We tried a number of further counterfactual hypotheses, including 'demerging' the 1930 population by 1919 size ratios and by time-of-merger size ratios, but since in our pilot studies these alternatives produced almost exactly the same results as those reported in Table 5.1 we judged that further experimentation on these lines was not required.

If company A purchases company B for cash (which in the 1920s was a common method of acquisition), then the immediate effect is likely to be that the net assets and the market value of the new company $(A + B)$ will not be very different from the initial assets and valuation of company A. If this is so, then the organisations which result from mergers will appear to be smaller than their component parts. But this is to take a very short-term view. It is to be expected that in the longer run the independent company A would have run down its cash resources in other ways, while the merged company $(A + B)$ will probably take steps to increase its holdings: and in the long term it is unlikely that the capital structure of company $(A + B)$ will differ greatly from the sum of the capital structures of company A and company B separately. (Though merger is often used as a means of effecting rapid changes in capital structure: when changes in the company tax system in 1965 increased the optimal debt-equity ratio, opportunities were extensively used in the subsequent merger boom to exchange equity for debt or pseudo-debt such as convertible loan stocks.) If these problems were serious, we would expect them to be reflected in significant discrepancies between the estimates obtained using the hypothetical merging and demerging procedures. No such discrepancies were found.

We have presented in Table 5.1 a large range of *CRN*s and numbers equivalent measures of concentration, but both the magnitude of concentration increase registered and the contribution of mergers to it appear much the same for all *CRN*s and for the whole relevant range of α.

In cases like this, even though there exists a catholic range of views among social scientists about what constitutes concentration, we can make an unequivocal statement about the direction, magnitude and source of concentration change. In the majority of our empirical studies our conclusions are similarly robust to a wide range of alternative views and to quote the results in such detail would clearly be unnecessary. Henceforth we will in many cases only quote the results for one appropriate CRN and two values of the elasticity parameter: $\alpha = 1$, which corresponds to entropy, and $\alpha = 2$, corresponding to the Herfindahl index.

Table 5.2 presents our results for 1919–30 in this abbreviated form, but now disaggregated by industry, according to the *Standard Industrial Classification* (Central Statistical Office 1958). (We have grouped the very small timber, clothing and leather industries into miscellaneous manufacturing: as noted in Chapter 4, the SIC has not been entirely successful in achieving comparable levels of disaggregation and the leather industry is insignificant in comparison with chemicals, food or non-electrical engineering.) The trends in the industry groups show a remarkable uniformity with our overall results: concentration increases in every group, and merger is the major force behind it in most groups. The main exception is the textile industry, where the CR10 and $\alpha = 2$ show merger as a relatively unimportant cause of rising concentration, whereas at $\alpha = 1$ (more precisely – though this is not shown in the Table – at all values below $\alpha = 1.4$) merger appears as the more important cause. This reflects the fact that the largest textile firms such as Courtaulds grew internally (Courtaulds' market value rose from £16m to £52m) and this is reflected in the CR10 and $\alpha = 2$. On the other hand medium-sized firms such as the Lancashire Cotton Corporation (an amalgamation of almost 100 firms, but still itself a small firm worth only £5m in 1930) and Combined Egyptian Mills (a merger of 15 firms worth £6m) – which are given greater weight at $\alpha = 1$ – owed their growth almost exclusively to merger activity. Our index faithfully reflects this ambiguity at different levels of α. Thus if we wished to say whether merger or internal growth was the more important source of rising concentration in textiles, we would be obliged to adopt a firmer view of what constitutes concentration.

Of course if we disaggregated our population further a number of other industries could be found in which internal growth made an important contribution to rising concentration: the car industry, which was innovating mass production technology in a rapidly growing market in the 1920s, would certainly be one of them. Nonetheless it is clear that the dominant cause of rising concentration, in manufacturing industries in general, was merger.

We have so far discussed the results for *relative* concentration, but Table 5.2 also provides the results for *absolute* concentration. We may see from the last cell of the table, that the total market value ('industry

TABLE 5.2. Sources of changes in relative and absolute concentration
Industry breakdown, 1919–30

SIC Industry group	Measure		1919	Change due to merger	Change due to internal growth	1930
III Food	CR10		52.9%	+ 30.7%	+ 1.5%	85.1%
	Numbers	$\alpha = 1$	35.7	− 25.9	− 0.5	9.3
	equivalent	$\alpha = 2$	15.2	− 11.3	− 0.8	3.1
	Industry size		£ 108m	–	+118%	£ 236m
	'Effective average' size of	$\alpha = 1$	£ 3.0m	+280%	+119%	£ 25.3m
	firm	$\alpha = 2$	£ 7.1m	+307%	+164%	£ 76.7m
IV Drink	CR10		35.0%	+ 9.6%	+ 8.0%	52.6%
	Numbers	$\alpha = 1$	96.9	− 37.2	− 12.6	47.1
	equivalent	$\alpha = 2$	40.2	− 13.0	− 7.5	19.7
	Industry size		£ 158m	–	+103%	£ 321m
	'Effective average' size of	$\alpha = 1$	£ 1.6m	+ 62%	+157%	£ 6.8m
	firm	$\alpha = 2$	£ 3.9m	+ 48%	+179%	£ 16.3m
V Tobacco	CR10		98.2%	+ 1.8%	–	100.0%
	Numbers	$\alpha = 1$	2.3	− 0.5	− 0.2	1.6
	equivalent	$\alpha = 2$	1.5	− 0.2	− 0.1	1.2
	Industry size		£ 278m	–	− 47%	£ 146m
	'Effective average' size of	$\alpha = 1$	£ 120.4m	+ 29%	− 41%	£ 92.4m
	firm	$\alpha = 2$	£ 190.0	+ 13%	− 45%	£ 117.3m
VI Chemicals	CR10		76.7%	+ 14.2%	+ 2.3%	93.2%
	Numbers	$\alpha = 1$	20.8	− 15.3	− 0.1	5.4
	equivalent	$\alpha = 2$	10.4	− 7.9	− 0.2	2.7
	Industry size		£ 95m	–	+ 38%	£ 131m
	'Effective average' size of	$\alpha = 1$	£ 4.6m	+256%	+ 48%	£ 24.2m
	firm	$\alpha = 2$	£ 9.1m	+291%	+ 37%	£ 48.8m
VII Metal Manufacture	CR10		44.3%	+ 17.2%	+ 3.9%	65.4%
	Numbers	$\alpha = 1$	60.1	− 33.1	− 3.5	23.5
	equivalent	$\alpha = 2$	34.6	− 16.0	− 3.1	15.5
	Industry size		£ 142m	–	− 16%	£ 118m
	'Effective average' size of	$\alpha = 1$	£ 2.4m	+123%	− 4%	£ 5.0m
	firm	$\alpha = 2$	£ 4.1m	+ 85%	+ 1%	£ 7.7m
VIII, Engineering IX, Vehicles and X, XI Shipbuilding	CR10		42.1%	+ 14.5%	− 8.0%	48.6%
	Numbers	$\alpha = 1$	76.4	− 33.6	+ 6.2	49.0
	equivalent	$\alpha = 2$	35.3	− 18.3	+ 11.6	28.6
	Industry size		£ 197m	–	+ 14%	£ 224m
	'Effective average' size of	$\alpha = 1$	£ 2.6m	+ 78%	− 0%	£ 4.6m
	firm	$\alpha = 2$	£ 5.6m	+107%	− 32%	£ 7.8m

SIC Industry group	Measure		1919	Change due to merger	Change due to internal growth	1930
XII Metal goods not elsewhere specified	CR10		68·0%	+ 12·8%	+ 6·3%	87·1%
	Numbers	$\alpha = 1$	22·1	− 7·3	− 2·6	12·2
	equivalent	$\alpha = 2$	16·9	− 4·5	− 3·2	9·2
	Industry size		£ 8m	−	+ 67%	£ 13m
	'Effective average' size of firm	$\alpha = 1$	£ 0·4m	+ 49%	+103%	£ 1·1m
		$\alpha = 2$	£ 0·5m	+ 37%	+122%	£ 1·5m
XIII Textiles	CR10		60·7%	+ 9·2%	+ 8·3%	78·2%
	Numbers	$\alpha = 1$	40·8	− 20·1	− 6·6	14·1
	equivalent	$\alpha = 2$	11·9	− 1·2	− 3·8	6·9
	Industry size		£ 177m	−	+ 8·5%	£ 192m
	'Effective average' size of firm	$\alpha = 1$	£ 4·4m	+ 97%	+ 59%	£ 13·6m
		$\alpha = 2$	£ 14·9m	+ 11%	+ 69%	£ 28·0m
XVI Building material	CR10		69·1%	+ 24·8%	+ 0·1%	94·0%
	Numbers	$\alpha = 1$	17·4	− 10·3	+ 0·0	7·1
	equivalent	$\alpha = 2$	6·1	− 1·9	+ 0·4	4·6
	Industry size		£ 24m	−	+ 73%	£ 42m
	'Effective average' size of firm	$\alpha = 1$	£ 1·4m	+147%	+ 73%	£ 5·9m
		$\alpha = 2$	£ 4·0m	+ 44%	+ 59%	£ 9·1m
XVII Paper and publishing	CR10		56·0%	+ 25·5%	+ 7·3%	88·8%
	Numbers	$\alpha = 1$	39·6	− 26·0	− 2·8	10·7
	equivalent	$\alpha = 2$	21·9	− 14·7	− 0·7	6·5
	Industry size		£ 49m	−	+ 82%	£ 89m
	'Effective average' size of firm	$\alpha = 1$	£ 1·2m	+193%	+128%	£ 8·3m
		$\alpha = 2$	£ 2·2m	+206%	+100%	£ 13·9m
XIV, Miscellaneous, XV, (including XVII, timber, XIX clothing and leather).	CR10		46·0%	+ 18·0%	+ 13·1%	77·1%
	Numbers	$\alpha = 1$	44·1	− 18·9	− 10·1	15·1
	equivalent	$\alpha = 2$	19·9	− 8·6	− 4·9	6·4
	Industry size		£ 47m	−	+ 68%	£ 80m
	'Effective average' size of firm	$\alpha = 1$	£ 1·1m	+ 75%	+179%	£ 5·3m
		$\alpha = 2$	£ 2·4m	+ 76%	+196%	£ 12·5m
III All − XIX Manufacturing Industries	CR50		43·4%	+ 13·9%	+ 6·4%	63·7%
	CR100		56·4%	+ 16·1%	+ 4·9%	77·4%
	Numbers	$\alpha = 1$	395	−212	− 48	135
	equivalent	$\alpha = 2$	144	− 73	− 27	44
	Industry size		£1033m	−	+ 54·1%	£1592m
	'Effective average' size of firm	$\alpha = 1$	£ 2·6m	+116%	+109%	£ 11·8m
		$\alpha = 2$	£ 7·2m	+103%	+149%	£ 36·9m

size') in 1919 of the manufacturing firms in our population was £1033m, and, since at α = 2 the number of 'equivalent equally sized firms' is 144, we can say that the 'effective average' size of firm is £7·2m. This 'effective average' is a more appealing measure than the familiar arithmetic mean, since the latter would be greatly affected by the number of small firms. For this reason it is particularly useful as a measure of differences in the sizes of 'typical' firms in different industries: thus it can be seen that, at α = 2, in 1919 the firms in the tobacco industry were largest (£19m) and those in the miscellaneous metal goods industry were smallest (£0·5m). Comparisons with 1930 show that, in manufacturing industry as a whole, the average size of firms more than quadrupled in this twelve year period, and, since share prices only rose by perhaps 15 %, this clearly represents a substantial real increase in the scale of enterprise. The increase in effective average size was especially marked in the food industry (× 9), where Unilever and other food firms were expanding rapidly, and in paper and publishing (× 6) where the press lords were actively building up their newspaper chains. The average firm increases its market value rather more than fourfold between 1919 and 1930. It slightly less than doubles its size through merger, and rather more than doubles its size through other factors. These factors include rising share prices over the period, so that it is likely that as far as real growth in the size of firms in these years is concerned, merger is on average a more significant factor than internal growth. This observation is reinforced by the certainty that part of the 'internal growth' of our population reflects acquisitions whose effect we have been unable to capture.

The finding that mergers were a major source of the rapidly rising concentration of the 1920s goes against the widely accepted view (see pp. 126–8, below) that before 1950 mergers were of little importance. It is, however, precisely what we should expect from the theoretical literature which stresses the constraints on internal growth. (Marx 1887, pp. 641–2; Penrose 1959, Chapter 8; Steindl 1965.) Moreover our findings also accord with the impression in Figure 5.1 that mergers were important in this period: the largest merger waves between 1900 and the later 1950s appear to have occurred in 1919–20 and 1926–9. A number of the largest firms of today – including I.C.I. and Unilever – owe their origins to founding mergers of these years, during which mergers accounted for a larger proportion of the total investment spending of firms than at any time before the 1960s (Hannah 1976). After these merger waves, however, merger activity subsided to relatively low levels and some earlier evidence has suggested that between the early 1930s and the mid 1950s concentration initially fell, and then recovered, so that overall there was little change in its level (Evely and Little 1960 and Figure 1.1). We therefore decided to carry out a similar exercise in this period in order, firstly, to check that this impression of low merger activity and little concentration change was correct and also to find out what the forces

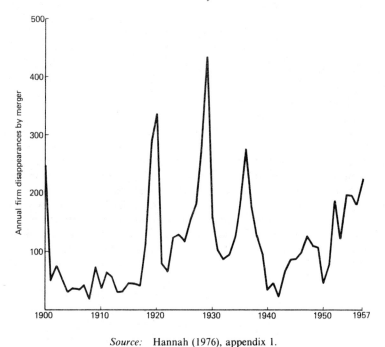

Source: Hannah (1976), appendix 1.

Fig. 5.1. Merger activity in U.K. manufacturing industry, 1900–57

behind concentration changes in individual industries in a period very different from the 1920s could be like.

Our populations for December 1930 and December 1948 were constructed in much the same way as those for our pilot study of 1919–30, with the market valuation of a company's capital, or some suitable approximation to it, as a measure of size. By 1948, however, data on a much wider range of companies was available and, since many of these first gained quotations in the 1930s, some estimate of their 1930 size could readily be made. As with our earlier work we ensured that every firm which appeared in 1930 also appeared in 1948 (and vice versa) unless it was clear that it genuinely had been founded or liquidated during the period: in that sense our population is a constant one, and comparisons between the two dates are meaningful. Direct comparison between the levels of concentration shown in this population and those shown in Tables 5.1 and 5.2 would, however, be invalid since our coverage of manufacturing industry has improved: our new 1930 population has almost four times as many firms and an aggregate market value a quarter higher than our earlier 1930 population. We estimate that our new population probably accounts for somewhat more than half of the total

TABLE 5.3 Sources of changes in relative and absolute concentration
Overall summary 1930–48

SIC Industry group	Measure	1930	Change due to merger	Change due to internal growth	1948
All Manufacturing	CR 50	54·3%	+ 1·6%	− 11·1%	44·8%
(III – XIX)	CR100	65·7%	+ 1·9%	− 10·7%	56·9%
	CR200	76·6%	+ 2·2%	− 9·0%	69·8%
	CR500	88·9%	+ 2·3%	− 4·6%	86·6%
Numbers equivalent					
	$\alpha = 0$	1998	− 428	+ 32	1602
	$\alpha = 0·6$	632	− 103	+ 187	716
	$\alpha = 0·8$	402	− 54	+ 177	525
	$\alpha = 1·0$	254	− 26	+ 152	380
	$\alpha = 1·2$	165	− 13	+123	275
	$\alpha = 1·4$	112	− 6	+ 96	202
	$\alpha = 1·6$	81	− 3	+ 75	153
	$\alpha = 1·8$	62	− 1	+ 59	120
	$\alpha = 2·0$	50	− 1	+ 48	97
	$\alpha = 2·5$	34	− 0	+ 32	66
Effective average size of firm					
	$\alpha = 1·0$	£ 7·9m	+ 12%	+ 34%	£ 11·8m
	$\alpha = 2·0$	£ 39·9m	+ 2%	+ 14%	£ 46·0m

profits made in manufacturing industry and that its coverage may have declined slightly over the period.

The results for manufacturing industry as a whole are shown in Table 5.3 and for individual industries in Table 5.4. These clearly confirm the view that concentration declined during the 1930s and 1940s. For manufacturing as a whole the CR100 falls from 65·7% to 56·9% and at $\alpha = 1$ and $\alpha = 2$ the number of 'equivalent equally-sized firms' rises substantially. In almost all of the industry groups, stagnant or falling concentration is indicated, the major exception being the drink industry, where the continued growth of Distillers offsets opposing tendencies and ensures that concentration rises slightly. The rise in the average size of firm for manufacturing as a whole is small in comparison to that registered for 1919–30 and, if we allow for the rise in share prices over this period of 79% (Moodies 1976), it is more properly characterised as a decline. Merger increases the average size of smallish firms by 10%–20% and affects large firms hardly at all.

The declines in concentration suggested by the data in Table 5.3 are surprisingly large, and we were rather less ready to take them at their face

TABLE 5.4. Sources of change in relative and absolute concentration
Industry breakdown, 1930–48

SIC Industry group	Measure	1930	Change due to merger	Change due to internal growth	1948
III Food	CR10	75·9%	+ 0·7%	− 6·1%	70·5%
	Numbers $\alpha = 1$	13·7	− 1·2	+ 7·7	20·2
	equivalent $\alpha = 2$	3·9	− 0·1	+ 3·0	6·8
	Industry size	£264·7m	–	+ 93%	£512·1m
	'Effective $\alpha = 1$	£ 19·3m	+10%	+ 20%	£ 25·4m
	average' size of				
	firm $\alpha = 2$	£ 67·9m	+ 1%	+ 10%	£ 75·3m
IV Drink	CR10	48·4%	+ 4·0%	− 3·2%	49·2%
	Numbers $\alpha = 1$	62·5	− 8·7	+ 1·4	55·2
	equivalent $\alpha = 2$	23·2	− 0·9	− 3·7	18·6
	Industry size	£349·5m	–	+ 95%	£667·9m
	'Effective $\alpha = 1$	£ 5·6m	+16%	+ 90%	£ 12·3m
	average' size of				
	firm $\alpha = 2$	£ 15·1m	+ 4%	+133%	£ 36·6m
V Tobacco	CR10	99·6%	+ 0·2%	− 0·3%	99·5%
	Numbers $\alpha = 1$	1·5	− 0	+ 0·9	2·4
	equivalent $\alpha = 2$	1·2	− 0	+ 0·4	1·6
	Industry size	£214·9m	–	+ 51%	£323·5m
	'Effective $\alpha = 1$	£140·6m	+ 1%	− 3%	£137·1m
	average' size of				
	firm $\alpha = 2$	£180·6m	+ 0	+ 15%	£208·7m
VI Chemicals	CR10	78·8%	+ 4·8%	− 6·4%	77·2%
	Numbers $\alpha = 1$	12·6	− 2·5	+ 4·1	14·2
	equivalent $\alpha = 2$	4·0	− 0·3	+ 1·1	4·8
	Industry size	£160·6m	–	+180%	£450·0m
	'Effective $\alpha = 1$	£ 12·7m	+26%	+ 97%	£ 31·6m
	average' size of				
	firm $\alpha = 2$	£ 40·0m	+10%	+114%	£ 94·2m
VII Metal Manufacture	CR10	50·8%	+ 3·8%	− 6·2%	48·4%
	Numbers $\alpha = 1$	45·0	− 5·5	+ 6·6	46·1
	equivalent $\alpha = 2$	25·0	− 1·2	+ 6·6	30·4
	Industry size	£158·0m	–	+188%	£455·3m
	'Effective $\alpha = 1$	£ 3·5m	−15%	+231%	£ 9·9m
	average' size of				
	firm $\alpha = 2$	£ 6·3m	+ 5%	+126%	£ 15·0m

SIC Industry group	Measure		1930	Change due to merger	Change due to internal growth	1948
VIII Non-Electrical Engineering	CR10		47·1%	+ 2·3%	− 17·9%	31·5%
	Numbers equivalent	$\alpha = 1$	64·4	− 6·6	+ 34·9	92·7
		$\alpha = 2$	23·9	− 0·9	+ 28·9	51·9
	Industry size		£ 75·9m	–	+219%	£242·5m
	'Effective average' size of firm	$\alpha = 1$	£ 1·2m	+ 11%	+100%	£ 2·6m
		$\alpha = 2$	£ 3·2m	+ 3%	+ 42%	£ 4·7m
IX Electrical Engineering	CR10		60·9%	+ 7·1%	− 8·2%	59·8%
	Numbers equivalent	$\alpha = 1$	32·6	− 8·0	+ 11·5	36·1
		$\alpha = 2$	19·1	− 4·8	+ 5·6	19·9
	Industry size		£103·7m	–	+134%	£242·8m
	'Effective average' size of firm	$\alpha = 1$	£ 3·2m	+32%	+ 60%	£ 6·7m
		$\alpha = 2$	£ 5·4m	+34%	+ 68%	£ 12·2m
X Shipbuilding	CR10		93·7%	+ 2·2%	− 4·9%	91·0%
	Numbers equivalent	$\alpha = 1$	5·5	− 0·7	+ 2·7	7·5
		$\alpha = 2$	2·8	− 0·2	+ 1·4	4·0
	Industry size		£ 34·3	–	+146%	£ 84·9m
	'Effective average' size of firm	$\alpha = 1$	£ 6·1m	+13%	+ 64%	£ 11·4m
		$\alpha = 2$	£ 12·1m	+ 6%	+ 67%	£ 21·3m
XI Vehicles and Aircraft	CR10		60·4%	+ 5·3%	− 14·8%	50·9%
	Numbers equivalent	$\alpha = 1$	32·3	− 4·8	+ 13·6%	41·1
		$\alpha = 2$	13·6	− 0·6	+ 10·7	23·7
	Industry size		£ 61·1m	–	+258%	£218·5m
	'Effective average' size of firm	$\alpha = 1$	£ 1·9m	+17%	+140%	£ 5·3m
		$\alpha = 2$	£ 4·5m	+ 5%	+ 96%	£ 9·2m
XII Metal Goods n.e.s.	CR10		53·7%	+ 4·2%	− 4·2%	53·7%
	Numbers equivalent	$\alpha = 1$	38·5	− 5·0	+ 2·2	35·7
		$\alpha = 2$	22·0	− 3·1	− 1·4	17·5
	Industry size		£ 19·6m	–	+246%	£ 67·9m
	'Effective average' size of firm	$\alpha = 1$	£ 0·5m	+15%	+224%	£ 1·9m
		$\alpha = 2$	£ 0·9m	+16%	+274%	£ 3·9m
XIII Textiles	CR10		65·7%	+ 0·1%	− 18·4%	47·4%
	Numbers equivalent	$\alpha = 1$	28·8	− 1·0	+ 28·6	56·4
		$\alpha = 2$	9·7	− 0	+ 11·5	21·2

SIC Industry group	Measure		1930	Change due to merger	Change due to internal growth	1948
	Industry size		£228·4m	–	+ 80%	£411·3m
	'Effective average' size of firm	α = 1	£ 7·9m	+ 4%	− 13%	£ 7·3m
		α = 2	£ 23·5m	+ 0%	− 18%	£ 19·4m
XVI Building Materials	CR10		61·7%	+ 6·4%	− 5·0%	63·1%
	Numbers equivalent	α = 1	33·4	− 8·1	+ 6·0	31·3
		α = 2	11·5	− 1·3	+ 4·1	14·3
	Industry size		£ 67·9m	–	+143%	£165·5m
	'Effective average' size of firm	α = 1	£ 2·0	+30%	+100%	£ 5·3m
		α = 2	£ 5·9m	+12%	+ 76%	£ 11·6m
XVII Paper and Publishing	CR10		70·5%	− 3·5%	− 13·1%	53·9%
	Numbers equivalent	α = 1	24·7	+ 2·6	+ 15·2	42·5
		α = 2	10·2	+ 3·0	+ 10·1	23·3
	Industry size		£115·6m	–	+107%	£255·1m
	'Effective average' size of firm	α = 1	£ 4·7m	− 9%	+ 41%	£ 6·0m
		α = 2	£ 11·3m	−22%	+ 20%	£ 11·0m
XIV, Miscellaneous XV, (including XVII, timber, XIX clothing and leather)	CR10		56·1%	+ 1·7%	− 11·2%	46·6%
	Numbers equivalent	α = 1	53·1	− 4·1	+ 25·9	74·9
		α = 2	15·4	− 0·3	+ 8·7	23·8
	Industry size		£142·2m	–	+139%	£339·5m
	'Effective average' size of firm	α = 1	£ 2·7m	+ 8%	+ 57%	£ 4·5m
		α = 2	£ 9·2m	+ 2%	+ 51%	£ 14·3m

value than was the case for the period 1919–30. Our most serious doubts were raised by our knowledge of changes occurring in the lower tail of smaller manufacturing firms which are not included in our populations – firms which still occupied an important place in the economy but which we were unable to include because, since they were unquoted, we had no direct information on the market value of their assets. In the earlier 1919–30 period, it seemed that the tendency towards higher concentration in the upper tail which we measured was likely to have been reinforced by increasing concentration in the lower part of the distribution, at least after 1924 (Bolton Committee 1971, pp. 58–60). In this case no problem arose from focusing attention on the upper tail. In 1930–48, by contrast, there is good reason to believe that the upper and lower tail of the distributions behaved differently. Among smaller firms the decline in total numbers and the consolidation of their assets into larger groupings appears to have proceeded apace. Although precise figures on the number of small *firms* are not available, the number of small *plants* (those employing 200 people or less) fell from 164,000 in 1930 to 144,000 in 1935 and 103,000 in 1948. Since there were 136,000 small *firms* (employing 200 people or less) in 1935, we might extrapolate from the data on *plants*, and guess that the number of small firms declined from around 150,000 in 1930 to around 100,000 in 1948. At the same time we know that the share of small *plants* in manufacturing net output declined from 40 % in 1930 to 37 % in 1948. These trends in the lower tail thus went directly against the trends in the upper tail which made for declining concentration.

We therefore decided to obtain a rough estimate of the extent to which the results of Table 5.3 would be modified if our population had been more comprehensive. We added to our population of 1930 2000 medium-sized firms sharing 15 % of the market, and a further 150,000 firms with a total share of 35 %. To our 1948 population we added 2000 medium and 110,000 small firms altering their shares of the total to 17 % and 33 % respectively. The results are shown in Table 5.5. We would make no claim to precision for these results – for our approximation of the lower tail could readily be criticised and improved upon – but the results do give us some indication of the possible effect of our omissions. At most values of α, the upper tail of firms (on which we based our results in Table 5.3) also dominate the results in Table 5.5 and concentration falls. For α = 0·8 and α = 0·6, however, concentration is shown as increasing. This reflects, we would claim, a real phenomenon, and helps to explain the disagreement (cf. Hall 1952, pp. 404–5; Hart and Prais 1956) about whether concentration really did fall in this period: for there is a genuine ambiguity about the direction of change. While larger firms

TABLE 5.5. Changes in concentration in manufacturing industry (including smaller and unquoted companies), 1930–48

		1930	*1948*
Numbers	α = 0·6	52,895	40,682
equivalent	α = 0·8	24,284	21,005
	α = 1·0	8,718	8,993
	α = 1·2	2,735	3,876
	α = 1·4	1,101	1,853
	α = 1·6	496	915
	α = 1·8	293	557
	α = 2·0	200	389

were losing ground, the tendency towards the elimination of very small firms, already evident in the 1920s, was sustained throughout the 1930s and 1940s among the firms in the lower part of the distribution, which receive greater emphasis for the lower values of α. Whether or not one views this as an overall rise or an overall decline in concentration must depend on one's view of the elasticity parameter α – on one's view, that is, of what exactly *is* important in a size distribution of firms.

A possible further qualification to our results for the upper tail is that the decline in concentration may have been exaggerated by our choice of the market valuation of a company's capital as a measure of its size. In 1930 large-scale enterprise was still very much in vogue and the market believed that large companies could weather the depression successfully. But, in the course of the next two decades, a number of well-managed smaller and medium-sized companies came to the market and their market rating improved, while in the wartime and immediately postwar periods the rating of large firms appears to have suffered more from government controls (and perhaps from a generalised fear of nationalisation) than that of smaller firms. Between December 1930 and December 1948, the Financial Times Industrial Ordinary share indexes (spliced at 1935), which are made up mainly of large companies, rose by 67%; whereas Moodies' 60 share index, in which half the weight is allocated to small and medium-sized firms, rose by 79% (Financial Times 1976; Moodies 1976). It might be argued, then, that the changes in relative size of large and small companies which we have measured are merely reflections of changed market sentiment and not of any real underlying change in the share of industry controlled by large and small companies. On the whole, however, we incline to the view that such long-run changes in stock exchange sentiment – and the change was a gradual and sustained one – could not have persisted unless they reflected real forces. Several arguments reinforce this view. The total market values of our population rose by 125% over this period so that comparison with either share index would suggest a good deal of real growth in capital. Casual inspection of our data suggests that the greater part of this new capital was raised by firms other than the largest in our population and hence that their real capital assets were increasing more rapidly than those of large companies. Furthermore there is independent evidence from estimates of changes in the share of the largest 50 firms in profits between 1938 and 1950 (Hart 1960) and of changes in the share of the largest 100 firms in net output between 1935 and 1948 (Prais, reported in Hannah 1976, appendix 2), that the position of the leading firms was being seriously eroded in these years. We conclude, then, that the results in Table 5.3 may be taken to reflect with reasonable accuracy actual changes in the level of concentration in the upper tail of the distribution between 1930 and 1948.

It remains, then, to examine the reasons why the large companies, many of them dating their rise to the merger boom of the 1920s, did not sustain their advance over the next two decades. Table 5.3 indicates that the answer is to be found in the reduced importance of merger activity in this period and the casual impression of Figure 5.1 is to that extent confirmed. Merger still tended to increase concentration (with the major exception of the paper and publishing industry where the break up of some newspaper groups and the sale of papermaking subsidiaries to a new entrant, Bowater, resulted in a decline in concentration) but in all industries the impact of merger was less than in 1919–30. At the CR100, for example, mergers had contributed a 16·1 percentage point rise in manufacturing industry as a whole in 1919–30; between 1930 and 1948 their contribution was only 1·9 percentage points. The average size of firm doubled through merger between 1919 and 1930; but in the next eighteen years it grew by only 10% or so from this source. Internal growth, by contrast, which in some industries in 1919–30 had reinforced the concentration-increasing effect of merger, now worked almost uniformly in the direction of reducing concentration. At the CR100, the 10·7 percentage point reduction due to internal growth swamps the 1·9 percentage point increase due to merger, producing a substantial net decline in concentration in manufacturing as a whole. The rapid internal growth of the medium-sized firms in engineering accounts for a good deal of the overall decline in concentration. But it is not only in the rapidly expanding industries that internal growth works to reduce concentration: the declining textile industry, for example, shows a decline both in the average size of firm and in relative concentration. (Even in the drinks industry, where the tied-house system maintained a strong incentive to merger, internal growth worked to reduce concentration at $\alpha = 1$, though the internal growth of one leading company, Distillers, ensures that it increases concentration at $\alpha = 2$.) We may provisionally conclude that, far from being a fundamental tendency in the economy in the period 1919–48, rising concentration was primarily a function of the level of merger activity, and that the internal expansion of firms worked in the direction of reducing concentration.

What were the motives for the surrender by large companies of the high market shares they held at the beginning of the period? As Stigler has argued (1968, chapter 13), merger for monopoly, followed by the imposition of high prices and restricted output and the gradual loss of sales to new or expanding rivals (attracted by the excess profits available) is a rational profit maximising strategy for the leading firm. But, while there may in some instances be no alternative to this course, a monopolist will generally seek to serve the interests both of his firm and its managers by preventing, as far as possible, the expansion of competition: and the contemporary evidence on cartels indicates that large firms were rather anxious to maintain their market shares in the increasingly common trade association agreements which they dominated (Lucas 1937). Thus we doubt that this argument can supply more than a small part of the answer: more significant may be the difficulties of managing the greatly enlarged enterprises created in the merger waves of 1919–30. Contemporaries laid great stress on the role of managerial diseconomies in limiting the scale of enterprise (Hannah 1974b), and a number of the leading firms are known to have experienced managerial difficulties in this period. As a result there was considerable hiving-off of assets – newspaper groups sold their paper mills, shipbuilding firms their steelworks – thus easing managerial problems, as well as reducing overall concentration. Some large firms appear to have attempted to minimise their managerial difficulties also by concentrating their production in fewer, larger plants: thus, despite declining concentration among *firms*, the number of large plants (those with 1500 or more employees) rose from 277 to 492 between 1930 and 1948 (Department of Employment 1971, p. 408). Some giants also introduced decentralised multidivisional management systems to cope with the problems of size. Firms which were unable to make these adjustments generally stagnated. Courtaulds, for example, with its conservative management (Coleman 1969), was worth very little more in 1948 than it had been in 1930, though its smaller rival in the rayon industry, British Celanese, had more than tripled in value. But even where managerial innovations enabled a giant firm to manage its existing assets relatively efficiently, it was not always as successful in developing new markets as smaller, more flexible rivals. I.C.I., for example, which had successfully introduced a multi-divisional management system and raised £15.25m new capital in 1929, was led by a politically inspired technological dream of serving empire fertiliser markets (which simply did not exist) to invest most of it in expensive new high pressure technology plant at Billingham: the investment was a disaster, most of the capital being written off during the 1930s (Reader 1975). I.C.I. was also slow to reap the new growth opportunities offered by the nascent plastics industry. By 1948, therefore, its market share had failed to live up to the promise of its earlier growth.

Special factors operating as a result of the increasing government control of the economy may also have weakened the position of large firms. Allocation of raw materials, which continued into peacetime years, was usually fixed on the basis of 1939 market shares, and the wartime concentration of production policy (by which some firms were closed, or converted to war work) was accompanied by promises that market shares would be restored after the war (Evely and Little 1960; Wiles 1952). The men who administered these controls, however, were often the leading directors of large firms – a logical outcome of the *rapport* between the bureaucrats of government and the technocrats of business which we have described in Chapter 3 – and it seems likely that their own firms observed the spirit of the controls and of profit limitation more punctiliously than did the smaller, entrepreneurial enterprises, (e.g.

Alford 1973, p. 414). Price controls were also more effective on the branded goods markets in which the leading firms were dominant; and, more generally, the sellers' market which existed in an era of widespread shortages and rationing weakened the impact of those aspects of marketing strategy – particularly large-scale advertising – in which the larger firms could be said to have had a competitive advantage. The decline in the market value of large firms relative to those of smaller and medium-sized companies appears, then, to have its origins partly in the underlying difficulties of the managers of the giants created in the earlier merger waves, and partly in the temporary disadvantages imposed upon them in the exceptional conditions of the 1940s.

The experience of large companies in the years after 1948 provides some confirmation of the view that some of the decline in their market share between 1930 and 1948 may have been due to special and temporary factors. We have not conducted a detailed empirical analysis of the sources of concentration change in the period 1948–57 in the manner of our studies of the two earlier periods. Nonetheless it is possible to discern the broad outlines from existing published studies. The share of the largest 100 firms in manufacturing net output rose rapidly to regain its 1930 level of 26 % by 1953 and a record level of 33 % by 1958. (Figure 1.1, p. 3 above). Similar upward movements were registered in individual industries: between 1951 and 1958 the proportion of (3 digit) industries in which the CR3 exceeded 50 % of net output almost doubled (Shepherd 1966; Armstrong and Silberston 1965). This rate of concentration increase compares with that registered for 1919–30, but, as Figure 5.1 suggests, it was not accompanied by a similarly intense merger wave. Indeed mergers can explain very little of the rise, for they accounted for less than 10 % of total investment spending between 1948 and 1957, a lower proportion than in any of the previous five decades (Hannah 1976). This rapid rise in concentration, in the absence of intense merger activity, suggests that special factors were at work and that the severely depressed condition of large companies in 1948 was an exceptional and temporary phenomenon. Their recovery was certainly rapid. I.C.I., for example, raised an extra £40m between 1948 and 1950 and by the latter date was coming to terms with some of its managerial problems (Reader 1975). More generally those large firms in the consumer goods industries, which had continued to advertise their products in the war (even though their goods could not be supplied!), reaped the benefit of accumulated customer goodwill when controls were relaxed, and the wartime sellers' market gave way to the buyers' market of the 1950s. Already, then, before the Restrictive Trade Practices Act of 1956 began to restrict the operation of the cartels of the 1930s which had tended to stabilise market shares, competitive pressures were substantially increased, and it seems that in this period large firms performed relatively well in response (Prais 1957).

In conclusion, then, there can be no doubt that there was, over the first six decades of the twentieth century, an increase in concentration, but close inspection of the sub-periods reveals no fundamental underlying trend to suggest that it was a gradual, continuing process. The effective average size of firm certainly increased, but so also did market size, and over many years the internal growth of smaller and medium-sized firms proved to have a powerful deconcentrating effect in many industries. Moreover if we accept the view that the rise of the modern corporate economy can be dated to the period of the 1920s, by which time much of the concentration increase had occurred (Hannah 1976), the behaviour of the corporate economy in subsequent decades provides little support to the view, widely expressed by economists of all shades of opinion, that continually increasing concentration is part of the natural order of things. If Engels was correct in expressing the view (in his additions to Marx's *Capital*) that 'the limit [of concentration of capital] would not be reached until the moment when the entire social capital was united in the hands either of a single capitalist or of a single capitalist company' (Marx 1887, p. 822), then that moment, on our evidence, would be a long time coming. This view could only be sustained if the exceptional 1920s, rather than other decades of the century, proved to be the harbinger of the future.

6 The Recent Experience – 1957–76

The 1960s saw the most substantial wave of merger activity the British economy had experienced since the 1920s. As Figure 6.1 shows, the annual value of acquisitions increased sharply after the early 1950s, culminating in the spectacular merger wave of 1967–9 which brought together G.E.C., A.E.I. and English Electric; British Motor Corporation and Leyland; created the giant Bass Charrington brewing chain; and generated proposals (subsequently abandoned) for a massive Unilever-Allied Breweries merger to create an industrial giant in the food and drink industries. During recent decades, also, merger has caught the popular imagination as never before. The contested takeover bid, where would-be acquirers appealed directly to shareholders over the heads of a hostile management, was almost unknown before the fifties. It was still very unusual in the fifties and sixties, accounting for only a tiny fraction of all merger activity, but instances of it would generate news headlines for weeks as the battles of I.C.I. to win control of Courtaulds or of G.E.C. to acquire A.E.I. developed. Firms discovered that their own shares were as acceptable a currency as cash in these takeover activities, and the proportion of the consideration for acquisition that took this form increased steadily (Kuehn 1975), facilitating explosive growth by a number of small firms as it became much easier to acquire firms of size comparable in magnitude to that of the acquirer. Although the government in 1965 obtained power to restrain merger by reference to the Monopolies Commission, its role was more typically encouraging or enthusiastic, as the continuing failure of macroeconomic policy to improve British economic performance prompted a search for micro-economic solutions. One caustic American observer (Caves 1968) tellingly caricatured the policy as: 'in order to achieve industrial efficiency, find the most efficient firm in Britain and merge the rest of them into it'. Government policy towards restrictive practices also indirectly encouraged merger, as an alternative to the cartels which had restricted competition in many British markets but were now increasingly viewed with disfavour (Elliott and Gribbin 1975).

What was the effect of these developments on industrial structure? We sought to appraise them using the same techniques as those we had applied to our historical data. As a measure of size, however, we used net

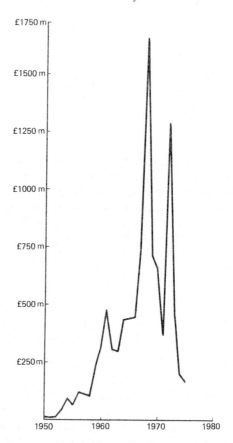

Sources: Hannah (1976), *Business Monitor M7*

Fig. 6.1. Merger activity in U.K. manufacturing industry, 1950–75

assets, employing the standardised accounting data compiled by the Board of Trade. Our basic population consisted of all quoted firms in manufacturing industry principally operating in the U.K. with 1957 assets in excess of £1m. To avoid bias due to the exclusion of rapidly growing firms, we added to this group all firms not already included which in the 1969 Board of Trade population had assets exceeding £2m. We also included a number of unquoted or foreign-owned companies for which similar data were available, and some firms which, although not classified as manufacturers by the Board of Trade (or its successors), had or acquired substantial manufacturing interests. Again this population necessarily excludes large numbers of small firms, and some of its growth will reflect the acquisition of these small firms: but it probably accounts for about two-thirds of all U.K. manufacturing activity in the period. We excluded completely those steel firms nationalised in 1967. The effect of this is discussed further below.

We noted in Chapter 4 some problems in using assets as a measure of size. One difficulty arises specifically from the effect of merger. If a company purchases another for a price that exceeds the book value of its assets (and this is increasingly common: Aaronovitch and Sawyer, 1975, p. 180) then accounting practice normally treats the difference as an intangible asset of the enlarged company. This means that if assets are used as a measure of size, 'synergy' – growth which is more than the addition of the two sets of assets – is likely to emerge simply from double entry book-keeping. If firm *A*, with book value £100, buys company *B*, of book value £50, for £75, then the new company will have book value of £175. The extreme instance of this is the appearance of Grand Metropolitan as third largest company in 1973 with assets of £800m of which nearly £300m arise from this source. Ironically the major part of this is the 'goodwill' of brewer Watneys, a brand name widely regarded as of little if not negative value (CAMRA 1974). If this were a serious problem in the period 1957–69, we should expect to get different answers in our 'merged 1957' calculation than those we obtain by 'demerging 1969'. This is not the case, but the difficulty may well be greater in future studies of this kind.

The aggregate results are presented in Table 6.1. As all casual observation would suggest, concentration increased substantially during the period, and this result is quite unambiguous. The CR10 rises from 24·6% to 27·1%, the share of the 100 largest from 60·1% to 74·9%. The equivalent number of firms at $\alpha = 1$ falls from 324 to 187, at $\alpha = 2$ from 92 to 71. Although this is a very large increase in concentration, it is interesting to note that it is not on the same scale as the rise which occurred in the 1920s. The share of the top ten firms in that population almost doubled, from 20% to 38%, and the top 100 began with 56·4% and ended with 77·4%. We likened the change in industrial structure in the 1920s to the exit from industry of two-thirds of all existing firms – a staggering and clearly unsustainable rate of change. The increase which we observe in the 1957–69 period, though clearly smaller, is rather more sensitive to the choice of measure. At $\alpha = 1$, which gives relatively greater emphasis to smaller firms, the number of equivalent firms falls by almost one half: at $\alpha = 2$, the decline is only about a quarter.

In Table 6.1 we also show the effect of mergers during the period. Between 1919 and 1930, merger and internal growth were working in the same direction: large firms were consolidating and improving their position not only through external growth but also through self-generated expansion. In the later period, however, the picture is very different. At all values of α, merger accounts for over 100% of the

TABLE 6.1. Aggregate concentration 1957–69

Measure	1957	Change due to merger	Change due to internal growth	1969
CRN (per cent)				
N = 50	48·4	+ 14·2	− 2·0	60·6
N = 100	60·1	+ 15·2	− 0·4	74·9
N = 200	73·0	+ 13·6	− 0·4	86·2
N = 500	88·9	+ 8·4	− 0·3	97·0
Numbers equivalent				
α = 0	1182	− 439	+ 1	744
α = 0·6	580	− 268	+ 14	326
α = 0·8	436	− 206	+ 15	245
α = 1·0	324	− 152	+ 14	187
α = 1·2	241	− 108	+ 13	146
α = 1·4	182	− 76	+ 12	118
α = 1·6	141	− 54	+ 10	97
α = 1·8	112	− 38	+ 8	82
α = 2·0	92	− 28	+ 6	71
α = 2·5	63	− 14	+ 3	52
Average size				
α = 1·0	£25·0m	+ 88%	+ 114%	£100·6m
α = 2·0	£87·6m	+ 43%	+ 112%	£265·8m

observed concentration increase. A similar pattern is reflected in the concentration ratios. The share of the top 50 firms rose from 48·4% in 1957 to 60·6% in 1969: but if all subsequent mergers had in fact occurred in 1957 the CR50 in that year would have been 62·6%. It was only the fact that the internally induced growth of large and merging firms was below the average of our population as a whole that prevented concentration from being higher than it was. The same tendencies are shown if we 'demerge' the 1969 population to undo the effects of the mergers which had so substantially changed it. Not only does such demerging reduce the 1969 concentration levels substantially, it reduces them below the levels which were in fact observed in 1957.

In our earlier period, then, it is probable that trends in both the capital and product markets were operating in similar directions. The stock market was reinforcing a tendency towards concentration into larger units which was in any case a result of expanding technological options and changing consumer choices, as mass production techniques gave larger producers a competitive edge. In more recent years, however, there is no evidence of anything of the kind. The preferences of consumers seem, if anything, to have favoured the small firm rather than the large: but any tendencies in this direction were swamped by the proclivity of the small firm to become absorbed into the large. This suggests a provisional conclusion that the fundamental tendency in this period, as between 1930 and 1948, was for internal growth to reduce concentration, with such deconcentration only prevented by intense merger activity. But this stronger conclusion depends on the accuracy of our hypothetical populations as descriptions of what would have happened in the absence of merger. The fact that the impact of internal growth on concentration is, in all periods, small relative to that of merger suggests that the errors in such descriptions are not large: but it might be argued that merger and internal growth are for large firms substitutes, so that acquisitions simply lead to patterns of growth which would have occurred, though no doubt more slowly, in any event.

For the individual firm the acquisition of another is an investment opportunity. The motivations which lead to external expansion are similar to those which prompt the purchase of new buildings, plant and machinery and the factors which govern an appraisal and constrain or encourage action are similar. It is well known that the economic variable which most successfully explains the level of merger activity is an index of share prices (Nelson 1959; Hannah 1972). There can be little doubt that share prices basically play the role of an expectational variable in this context: both market levels and the number of acquisitions are well correlated with investment intentions, direct measures of the state of business confidence and expenditure on readily available equipment such as vehicles (Mayer 1976). In 1973, when City and business opinion diverged sharply so that firms remained optimistic while share prices were falling, both investment activity and mergers remained high.

This association between external and internal growth does not, however, necessarily imply that one displaces the other. Clearly there is some potential conflict between them. Both demand managerial resources so that the acquiring firm is in a relatively unfavourable position to exploit new investment opportunities: while both are equally satisfactory in enhancing those components of managerial utility which are derived from the scale and rate of growth of the operations of the firm. Thus the Ford Motor Company has expanded its U.K. output and market share almost entirely from its own resources, while British Leyland, hampered by the problems of integrating the many formerly independent firms which it acquired, has been unable to generate internal growth on the scale which its competitor has achieved or its founders had hoped. But there are major differences between internal growth and growth through merger. An acquisition normally brings with it demand for the increased capacity which it provides, while the construction of new capacity does not. The former may therefore involve less risk for a given expansion; but its profitability will not be much enhanced by an increase in expected demand for output, while that of new plant will be. Further, new investment increases the capacity of the industry as a whole, while merger does not, so that any profitable opportunities which are available to firms generally are not reduced or eliminated by merger. Thus, while it is certainly possible that firms with extensive acquisition programmes are less likely to be engaged in programmes of new investment, empirical evidence does not suggest that such firms do in fact invest relatively less than those which make few takeovers (Meeks, forthcoming).

We doubt then that it is possible to argue generally that merger simply brings about reallocations of market shares which would have occurred in any case through internal growth. In the 1920s, when other forces were promoting increased concentration, it is probable that many of the effects of merger represented an acceleration of that trend. In the 1960s, when there is no sign of any other tendency in that direction, it seems much less likely that the increases in concentration which merger brought about would have happened in its absence. Of course, there are certainly particular instances of merger where this is clearly the case. One of the roles of merger in the corporate economy is as a 'civilised alternative to bankruptcy' (Dewey 1961). Firms concede to their rivals market shares, which they do not hope to maintain, by selling their assets. The work of Singh (1971) and Kuehn (1975) shows evidence of this type of merger: firms with exceptionally low profitability have a high propensity to be taken over. Yet it is also clear that very low profitability is not the major distinguishing characteristic of acquired firms. Overall, then, we think it very unlikely that there would have been a substantial increase in concentration in the period from 1957–69 had there been no merger boom in these years.

The pattern in individual industries is shown in Table 6.2. Only two industries fail to show increasing concentration over the period. Both of these give ambiguous results. In non-electrical engineering, a mild general tendency to increase is offset by the decline of the largest firm, Vickers, which not only performs relatively poorly over the period but relinquishes its aircraft interests to B.A.C. and its steel-making activities through nationalisation. In building materials the equivocal verdict on the direction of concentration increase is particularly interesting. A number of small firms in this industry – most conspicuously Redland and Ready Mixed Concrete – grow extremely rapidly. This brings into being companies more comparable in size to the dominant firm in the sector (A.P. Cement). On one view (indicated by $\alpha = 1$) the increased importance of relatively large firms raises concentration: on another (indicated by $\alpha = 2$) the building materials sector is no longer overshadowed by a single market leader.

In all other industries a uniform pattern is seen. Concentration increases: in some cases internal growth operates so as to effect marginal

TABLE 6.2. Sources of changes in relative and absolute concentration
Industry summary 1957–69

SIC Industry group	Measure	1957	Change due to merger	Change due to internal growth	1969
III Food	CR10	62·1%	+ 12·9%	+ 5·5%	80·5%
	Numbers $\alpha=1$	28·3	− 9·9	− 1·7	16·7
	equivalent $\alpha=2$	19·6	− 5·9	− 0·9	12·8
	Industry size	£ 525m	–	+171%	£1425m
	'Effective average' size of firm $\alpha=1$	£ 18·6m	+ 54%	+198%	£ 85·1m
	$\alpha=2$	£ 26·9m	+ 43%	+191%	£ 111·4m
IV Drink	CR10	40·8%	+ 45·4%	+ 1·0%	87·2%
	Numbers $\alpha=1$	55·7	− 41·6	− 0·4	13·7
	equivalent $\alpha=2$	23·5	− 14·5	+ 0·1	9·1
	Industry size	£ 751m	–	+158%	£1933m
	'Effective average' size of firm $\alpha=1$	£ 13·5m	+293%	+166%	£ 140·8m
	$\alpha=2$	£ 31·9m	+158%	+157%	£ 212·1m
V Tobacco	CR10	100·0%	–	–	100·0%
	Numbers $\alpha=1$	2·9	− 0·6	− 0·0	2·3
	equivalent $\alpha=2$	1·9	− 0·2	+ 0·0	1·8
	Industry size	£ 290m	–	+121%	£ 641m
	'Effective average' size of firm $\alpha=1$	£ 101·9m	+ 23%	+122%	£ 279·7m
	$\alpha=2$	£ 152·9m	+ 10%	+116%	£ 362·3m
VI Chemicals	CR10	80·6%	+ 2·0%	+ 3·8%	86·4%
	Numbers $\alpha=1$	10·6	− 2·3	+ 0·2	8·5
	equivalent $\alpha=2$	3·8	− 0·3	+ 0·1	3·6
	Industry size	£1098m	–	+156%	£2808m
	'Effective average' size of firm $\alpha=1$	£ 103·3m	+ 29%	+147%	£ 328·7m
	$\alpha=2$	£ 290·7m	+ 9%	+147%	£ 780·9m
VII Metal Manufacture	CR10	58·7%	+ 16·7%	− 1·1%	74·3%
	Numbers $\alpha=1$	28·8	− 15·9	+ 3·5	16·4
	equivalent $\alpha=2$	13·4	− 8·0	+ 2·5	7·9
	Industry size	£ 360m	–	+ 93%	£ 696m
	'Effective average' size of firm $\alpha=1$	£ 12·5m	+123%	+ 52%	£ 42·4m
	$\alpha=2$	£ 26·8m	+149%	+ 32%	£ 88·1m

SIC Industry group	Measure	1957	Change due to merger	Change due to internal growth	1969
VIII Non-Electrical Engineering	CR10	39·0%	+ 6·0%	− 12·9%	32·1%
	Numbers {α = 1	74·4	− 19·3	+ 21·7	76·8
	equivalent {α = 2	24·5	− 3·3	+ 27·5	48·7
	Industry size	£ 684m	−	+ 92%	£1317m
	'Effective average' size of firm {α = 1	£ 9·2m	+ 35%	+ 38%	£ 17·1m
	{α = 2	£ 27·9m	+ 16%	− 17%	£ 27·0m
IX Electrical Engineering	CR10	60·4%	+ 22·0%	− 1·2%	81·2%
	Numbers {α = 1	33·0	− 21·5	+ 4·0	15·5
	equivalent {α = 2	17·3	− 12·4	+ 2·9	7·8
	Industry size	£ 798m	−	+181%	£2240m
	'Effective average' size of firm {α = 1	£ 24·2m	+186%	+109%	£ 144·5m
	{α = 2	£ 46·1m	+251%	+ 76%	£ 285·6m
X Shipbuilding	CR10	80·3%	+ 10·5%	+ 2·5%	93·3%
	Numbers {α = 1	15·1	− 4·4	− 1·3	9·4
	equivalent {α = 2	10·7	− 2·4	− 1·5	6·8
	Industry size	£ 138m	−	+ 13%	£ 156m
	'Effective average' size of firm {α = 1	£ 9·2m	+ 39%	+ 31%	£ 16·6m
	{α = 2	£ 12·9m	+ 27%	+ 39%	£ 22·8m
XI Vehicles and Aircraft	CR10	67·2%	+ 20·0%	− 1·4%	85·8%
	Numbers {α = 1	25·7	− 14·2	+ 1·3	12·8
	equivalent {α = 2	15·7	− 8·6	+ 1·0	8·1
	Industry size	£ 622m	−	+136%	£1465m
	'Effective average' size of firm {α = 1	£ 24·2m	+123%	+112%	£ 114·9m
	{α = 2	£ 39·6m	+122%	+107%	£ 181·8m
XII Metal Goods n.e.s.	CR10	67·2%	+ 12·8%	− 2·9%	77·1%
	Numbers {α = 1	20·8	− 8·5	+ 2·5	14·8%
	equivalent {α = 2	6·5	− 1·8	+ 1·2	5·9
	Industry size	£ 381m	−	+110%	£ 800m
	'Effective average' size of firm {α = 1	£ 18·3m	+ 68%	+ 77%	£ 54·3m
	{α = 2	£ 58·1m	+ 35%	+ 71%	£ 134·0m
XIII Textiles	CR10	55·9%	+ 23·4%	− 5·1%	74·2%
	Numbers {α = 1	47·2	− 32·0	+ 2·4	17·6
	equivalent {α = 2	15·5	− 9·4	+ 0·6	6·7

SIC Industry group	Measure		1957	Change due to merger	Change due to internal growth	1969
	Industry size		£ 830m	–	+ 56%	£1292m
	'Effective average' size of firm	α = 1	£ 17·6m	+213%	+ 34%	£ 73·6m
		α = 2	£ 53·4m	+156%	+ 41%	£ 193·5m
XVI Building Materials	CR10		71·2%	+ 3·2%	– 9·4%	65·0%
	Numbers equivalent	α = 1	19·3	– 2·7	+ 1·3	17·9
		α = 2	9·0	+ 0·5	+ 2·1	11·6
	Industry size		£ 237m	–	+271%	£ 881m
	'Effective average' size of firm	α = 1	£ 12·3m	+ 25%	+219%	£ 49·1m
		α = 2	£ 26·3m	+ 2%	+184%	£ 76·2m
XVII Paper and Publishing	CR10		63·6%	+ 16·1%	– 1·6%	78·1%
	Numbers equivalent	α = 1	27·7	– 11·5	+ 1·3	17·4
		α = 2	11·3	– 2·9	+ 0·7	9·1
	Industry size		£ 554m	–	+135%	£1303m
	'Effective average' size of firm	α = 1	£ 20·0m	+ 72%	+118%	£ 75·0m
		α = 2	£ 48·9m	+ 35%	+116%	£ 142·8m
XIV, Miscellaneous XV, (including XVII, timber, XIX clothing and leather)	CR10		58·3%	+ 7·0%	+ 0·3%	65·6%
	Numbers equivalent	α = 1	35·8	– 9·2	+ 0·6	27·2
		α = 2	11·6	– 2·0	+ 0·9	10·5
	Industry size		£ 430m	–	+152%	£1081m
	'Effective average' size of firm	α = 1	£ 12·0m	+ 35%	+146%	£ 39·7m
		α = 2	£ 37·1m	+ 21%	+130%	£ 103·4m

increases; in more instances it would bring about marginal reductions, but in all cases it is clear that merger is the dominant influence on industrial structure. In three industries the increases are particularly striking. In drink, the average size of firm increased by 150% through merger between 1919 and 1930, and by a further 5%–15% between 1930 and 1948. In our most recent period the average size of surviving firms quadruples through merger: between two-thirds and three-quarters of all firms disappear in our numbers equivalent measures. This brings to an end the frenetic pace of amalgamation in this industry, since virtually all the few remaining small breweries are wholly or substantially family controlled companies set on maintaining independence – no opportunities for acquisition remain because all have already been exploited. In electrical engineering and textiles the extensive acquisition activities of particular firms (G.E.C. and Courtaulds respectively) are the major factor at work. The absolute concentration measures show substantial differences between industries in the average size of firm. Chemicals, food, drink and tobacco, electrical engineering and vehicles are characterised by large firms, while units in non electrical engineering, shipbuilding and building materials remain much smaller.

Our metal manufacture sector is a very attenuated one, and the absolute measures show a low average size of firm. This is because the major firms in the sector were nationalised during the period, and we have excluded both them and the British Steel Corporation which succeeded them from our calculations. This is in some respects an odd procedure, since the formation of British Steel was the largest merger and the most potent concentrating force in manufacturing industry during the period: but the manner in which it occurred, at any rate, was quite different from the other mergers whose effect we have analysed. We have, however, estimated for $\alpha = 1$ and $\alpha = 2$ the effect on our measures of supposing that B.S.C. had been formed by merger. The impact is of course substantial. At $\alpha = 1$, it amounts to perhaps a quarter of the concentration increase arising from other sources. At $\alpha = 2$, it is much greater, as is to be expected, since B.S.C. would have been the largest firm (in terms of net assets) in our population. The effect of this merger on this indicator, with its emphasis on the largest firms, is comparable in magnitude to that of all other mergers during the period.

The industry data in Table 6.2 cannot be used to make inferences about individual market concentration. The level of aggregation at which we are working is much too high for that to be possible. The three largest firms in the food industry, for example, are Unilever, Rank Hovis

TABLE 6.3. The effects of steel nationalisation on aggregate concentration

	1	2	3	4	5	6
	1957 population			1969 population excluding steel companies	Effect of B.S.C. on concentration (3–2)	Effect of other factors on concentration (4–1)
	excluding steel companies	including steel companies	assuming B.S.C. formed			
CR10	24·6%	23·4%	28·2%	27·1%	+ 4·8%	+ 2·5%
CR50	48·4%	49·1%	51·4%	60·6%	+ 2·3%	+ 12·2%
$\alpha = 1$	323·8	322·5	282·9	186·5	− 39·6	− 137·3
$\alpha = 2$	92·2	98·7	73·0	70·6	− 25·7	− 21·6

McDougall and Cadbury Schweppes, but the range of products over which they compete with each other is very small: equally two of them are substantially engaged in activities outside food, as a result of diversifications which did not in themselves affect concentration in the markets for individual products. However it is clear from studies at the 3-digit industry level that concentration in particular markets also showed a strong upward trend in the period, especially in those markets where merger activity was extensive. (Sawyer 1971; George 1975; Hart, Utton and Walshe 1973).

Whilst the level of aggregation is high, the similarity of trends in all industry groups remains a striking feature of Table 6.2; and this aspect is all the more impressive since it is true in each of the three periods we have examined. In the 1920s, concentration increased substantially on account of both merger and internal growth, and this was true in most industries. Between 1930 and 1948, it fell somewhat, and merger had little effect, and this was true in all major sectors. In the 1957–69 period, there was a further marked increase, wholly accounted for by merger, and again virtually all industries conform to this pattern. This evidence militates strongly against the view that increased concentration is a product of technical factors of a kind specific to particular sectors. It is very unlikely that the tide of increased scale economies ebbs and flows in all industries at the same times with quite this degree of regularity. It is possible that increasing concentration is influenced by technical developments common to *all* industries. In the 1920s, when mass production techniques were devised in many processes with quite distinct end uses, this makes some sense and may be a partial explanation. It is very difficult to think of any similar developments in the 1960s, and it seems more probable that the common factor was the enthusiasm of businessmen, stock market and government for growth by merger. The origins of this enthusiasm, and the justification for it, is a matter which we consider in more detail in Chapter 8.

After the great merger boom of 1967–9, the recorded number and value of acquisitions declined (Figure 6.1 above). We therefore extended our study, principally to see how the trend of aggregate concentration had been developing in the 1970s. A subsidiary objective was to make use of the wider range of information (on turnover, employment and employees' remuneration) which companies have been required to make available since 1967, to see how sensitive conclusions about levels of and changes in concentration were to the units in which size is measured. These objectives were to some extent in conflict. In order to allow meaningful comparisons we excluded from our population firms for which it was not possible to obtain satisfactory measures of size in all units: but we were able to include all large manufacturing firms with their principal ownership and operations in the U.K. The population basically consisted of all members of the D.T.I. set of listed companies with 1969 assets in excess of £2m, supplemented where appropriate, and in particular by those companies with 1973 assets over £2·5m. This included about 700 firms, which probably account for about two-thirds of U.K. net output in manufacturing.

TABLE 6.4. Changes in concentration using various measures of firm size, 1969–73

	Assets		Market value		Profits	
	1969	1973	1969	1973	1969	1973
CR10	30·9%	31·6%	32·8%	33·7%	32·8%	32·7%
CR50	65·0%	67·3%	65·9%	65·7%	63·5%	64·8%
$\alpha = 1$	157	145	149	149	160	147
$\alpha = 2$	57	57	57	61	53	52

	Turnover		Employment		Value added	
	1969	1973	1969	1973	1969	1973
CR10	32·6%	32·4%	26·1%	26·1%	28·5%	28·9%
CR50	63·6%	65·3%	55·8%	58·6%	57·9%	60·1%
$\alpha = 1$	165	148	216	196	202	183
$\alpha = 2$	55	52	89	88	78	78

The results are shown in Table 6.4, for six measures. These are net assets (defined as for 1957–69); market value (which here relates to equity capitalisation alone); trading profit (before interest); turnover (of U.K. operations but including exports); number of U.K. employees; and 'value added' (measured as the sum of trading profit before interest and employees' remuneration). (This latter measure has deficiencies. Perhaps the most serious is that the profits figure relates to world wide operations, whereas the figures given for employees' remuneration are attributable only to U.K. activities. Although it can be argued that this does reflect the contribution to GNP, it does not seem likely that this is what we are interested in for purposes of concentration measurement.) The relative magnitudes of the concentration indices conform broadly to expectations. The three measures of capital – net assets, market value and profits – give significantly higher levels of concentration at both dates than does employment, while value added lies somewhere between the two. That concentration of turnover should be so high, and in particular higher than value added, may at first appear surprising, since it suggests that large firms are less vertically integrated than small. The explanation for this lies mainly in the industrial distribution of large firms. They are prominent in industries such as food manufacture, which are relatively close to the consumer and have a low ratio of net to gross output: and less dominant in engineering, where intermediate goods are more commonly produced and where the ratio of the value added to gross output is generally higher (C.S.O. 1975a).

Although their levels are different, the trend of the various measures between 1969 and 1973 is very similar. There is little change in the Herfindahl index ($\alpha = 2$) with its emphasis on the largest firms: whereas there is a marked increase in concentration as indicated by entropy ($\alpha = 1$). The industrial giants of the late 1960s do not increase their dominance significantly: but relatively large companies continue to make gains in size at the expense of smaller firms. This pattern is confirmed in the behaviour of the concentration ratios: the CR10 remains roughly static while the CR50 and higher ratios increase sharply. We analysed the causes of this change in the usual way, by constructing a hypothetical merged distribution for 1969 (using value added). The results of this are shown in Table 6.5, and indicate that the conclusions drawn for the 1957–69 period appear to continue to hold in the early 1970s. Merger explains fully 100% of concentration increase. The changes in the Herfindahl index and the CR10 show that in the absence of merger the share of the largest firms would have shown a modest decline, but the (relatively few) major acquisitions over the period were sufficient to prevent this. The large number of small mergers during the period, mainly in 1972–3, account for all of the entropy-registered increase in concentration.

TABLE 6.5. Mergers and concentration, 1969–1973: (value added)

	1969	Merged 1969	1973
CR10	28·5%	29·2%	28·9%
CR50	57·9%	60·0%	60·1%
$\alpha = 1$	202	181	183
$\alpha = 2$	78	74	78

We were concerned to examine the extent to which the choice of measure affected our results in this period. It is worth noting that it is not necessary that alternative measures of the size of a particular firm should be well correlated with each other for levels of and trends in concentration as registered by particular measures to be similar. The degree of rank correlation observed is high but by no means perfect: as one illustration, the 'largest' firm under four of the six criteria is I.C.I. but turnover suggests Unilever and employment G.E.C. (1969) or B.L.M.C. (1973). Suppose there is some 'true' measure of size (e.g. value added), and all actual measures are estimates of this, subject to an independently distributed error term with mean zero. Then the Gibrat analysis can be applied to this problem, and it shows that all measures will overestimate the 'true' measure of concentration, and the greater the variance of the error term the greater the overestimate will be. Thus two measures can both have substantial variances of errors, and hence be poorly correlated with each other: yet provided the magnitude of the variances is similar they will yield much the same figures for concentration ratios and α concentration indices. Of course this model is an inadequate description of reality – since there are systematic relationships between factor intensity and firm size, the mean of the error-in-variable terms will be related to 'true' size. But it does give some insight into the processes underlying these results.

TABLE 6.6. Concentration as measured by market value, 1969–76

Indicator	1969	1973	1976
CR5	21·0%	21·1%	23·7%
CR10	32·8%	33·7%	34·0%
CR50	65·9%	65·7%	65·9%
CR100	78·9%	78·4%	80·9%
CR200	88·8%	88·7%	90·9%
$\alpha = 1$	149	149	134
$\alpha = 2$	57	61	49

One measure performs rather differently from the other five, and that is market value. This also happens to be the measure for which the most up-to-date information is available, and we have therefore extended our analysis to 1976 and give, in Table 6.6, the results over the whole period 1969–76. This data raises a number of interesting questions concerned both with the identification of recent trends in concentration and with the principles of concentration measurement.

First, what happened over this period? Our judgement is that concentration increased over the period, and that the increase principally occurred between 1969 and 1973. The market value figures for 1973 are in some respects misleading, and fail to show the trend of rising concentration shown by the other measures in Table 6.4. The end of 1973 was a time of some disorder in stock markets, when the simultaneous development of serious political and economic crises in Britain led to a sharp fall in prices on top of a rather more sustained downward drift, and the 1973 figures reflect various apparent reratings of particular companies and groups of companies which were not all maintained in the long run. One example of such changes is in the status of the largest firm, I.C.I., whose share in the 1969 population was 8·3%; this fell in 1973 to 6·3% but by 1976 had risen to almost 9·8%. Between 1969 and 1973 the *Times* index of large companies' share prices falls by about 5% while the corresponding small companies' index rises by a similar amount. However by 1976 this relative change in the share prices of large and small companies – which has a substantial effect on market value concentration measures – though not eliminated was much reduced. Much of the apparent increase in concentration between 1973 and 1976 is therefore probably a reflection of a re-establishment of market sentiment after an excessive reaction in 1973. As we have suggested above (p. 78), market values will only reliably reflect underlying changes in the long run; because of their anticipatory nature, changes in market values are more likely to record false steps than our other measures.

These observations are reinforced by the knowledge that merger – which we have shown to be the principal cause of concentration change – occurred on a much larger scale in 1969–73 (especially 1972) than in 1974–5 (Figure 6.1 above). But if these market value figures do give a valid indication of long-term trends (and the picture they show must still be viewed very tentatively) it seems likely that there was some tendency to deceleration of the movement to increased concentration in the 1970s. This most recent period is about half as long as that used in our 1957–69 study, but while in the earlier period the equivalent number of firms fell by 30%–50% (and almost certainly at a more rapid rate in the later part of the period), the reduction between 1969 and 1976 is in the region of 10%.

A second point is that the superiority of our comprehensive measures over the more conventional *CRN* is well illustrated in these figures. Over the period 1969–76, the CR50 (which is the measure we first computed) shows no change. Both α measures record a significant concentration increase, and the wider range of concentration ratios which we present in Table 6.6 show that this indication is correct. Although there is no change in the relative strengths of the top 50 firms, taken together, and the rest of the population, taken together, there are marked increases in concentration *within* these groups. There can be no real room for doubt that, comparing these distributions as a whole, concentration increased, although the magnitude of the change may depend on the aspects of concentration which particularly interest us. It appears, then, that there has not yet been a sustained reaction against large size comparable to that which was experienced in the 1930s and 1940s.

7 The Gibrat Effect

THE LAW OF PROPORTIONATE EFFECT

We begin this chapter by setting out a simple model of the growth of firms, normally ascribed to the French engineer Gibrat (1931) although it can be traced to Kapteyn (1903) and beyond. Suppose that in each period of time the probability that any particular firm will experience any particular growth rate is the same. Suppose that the growth performance of a firm in each period is independent of its performance in other periods: a fast-growing firm is no more or less likely than any other to grow more rapidly in subsequent years. And suppose that there is no single period which is so important in the life of firms as to remain a dominant influence on their fortunes indefinitely thereafter – there is no period whose effect cannot be thrown off, given sufficient time. If these three assumptions hold, the growth process conforms to what has become known as the Law of Proportionate Effect. The distribution of firms' sizes will tend over time to become lognormal, and the variance of this distribution will increase steadily. A lognormal distribution is one whose logarithms are normally distributed, and its characteristic skew shape is illustrated in Figure 7.1. Its properties are described in detail in Aitchison and Brown (1957), but the proposition outlined above is easy to check. If Z_t is the log of the size of a firm in period t, then the assumptions of the Law of Proportionate Effect imply that $Z_t = Z_o + X_1 + \ldots + X_t$, where Z_o is the log of the initial size of the firm and $X_t = \log (1 + g_t)$ with g_t the firm's growth rate in period t. Thus Z_o, $X_1 \ldots X_t$ are mutually independent random variables, and provided the

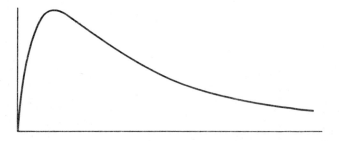

Fig. 7.1. Lognormal Distribution

variance of each is sufficiently small relative to their sum the central limit theorem implies that Z_t tends to normality for sufficiently large t.

This is not the only possible variant of the Law of Proportionate Effect. An alternative model is that of Champernowne (1953). For our assumption that all firms are equally likely to grow by the same proportion, Champernowne substitutes the formulation that the probability that a firm will grow from size class i to size class j depends only on the differences in relative positions of class i and class j. While this is very similar in spirit, it is identical only if the way in which firms are distributed within size classes is the same. (The relationship is discussed by Aitchison and Brown (1954).) It is somewhat different in effect, since the asymptotic distribution is no longer lognormal, but Pareto. This has the form

$$F(x) = 1 - \left(\frac{x_o}{x}\right)^\alpha$$

where $F(x)$ is the proportion of firms with size less than x, x_o the size of largest firm and α a slope parameter describing the distribution. Another possible modification is to allow for the possibility of births and deaths among firms: if this is done the Yule distribution (Simon and Bonini 1958) may be the result. While this may be regarded as a move towards realism, births are not clearly defined events in the lives of firms, and are in any case rather rare among firms of the size with which we are generally concerned in this volume.

These and other statistical distributions do in fact provide quite good approximations to the observed size distribution of firms, although the Pareto distribution is in general only of value in the upper part of the distribution. A survey by Quandt (1966), using a range of tests of goodness of fit, found several distributions (including lognormal and Pareto) acceptable, but was not able to discriminate decisively between them. This correspondence with reality is quite surprising, given the implausibility of the assumptions on which these models are based. It is worth remarking, however, that this implausibility is not as great as is sometimes suggested (e.g. Scherer 1970) – in particular, it is not implied that the growth of firms occurs by chance. Industrial success and failure is clearly not a random process, and the use of the word 'chance' in social sciences is simply a label for our ignorance. The model does assume, however, that the incidence of the factors which bring about growth and decline in each period is unrelated to the initial size of firm, and that hypothesis strains credulity enough. We might accept the assumption that no one period is decisive in the life of firms without too much difficulty, but the assumption which rules out correlation between growth in consecutive periods clearly cannot be maintained. It would be extraordinary if managements which achieve rapid growth at some time displayed no tendency whatever to continue it subsequently, and although there is some contrary opinion (Little and Rayner 1966), the empirical evidence suggests that they do (Singh and Whittington 1975).

However these assumptions are not all crucial to the conclusion of the model. As shown by Kalecki (1945), if there is a simple linear relationship between logs of growth and logs of firm's size, so that $Z_t = \beta Z_{t-1} + (1 - \beta)\overline{Z}$ for some β and $\overline{Z}$, induction shows that

$$Z_t = \overline{Z} + X_t + \beta X_{t-1} + \beta^2 X_{t-2} + \ldots + \beta^t X_o$$

Z_t remains the sum of independent random variables, and the distribution still tends to lognormality. In this model, concentration still increases over time, however rapid the rate of regression to the mean $\overline{Z}$ (i.e. however small β is), unless either the regression parameter β falls or the variance of growth rates falls over time. But even if these remain constant the rate of increase of concentration will diminish, and there is a limiting distribution of the sizes of firms with mean $\overline{Z}$ and variance $\theta^2/(1 - \beta^2)$, where θ^2 is the variance of growth rates in each individual period. Serial correlation of growth rates can be dealt with similarly. If, for example, we have

$$Z_t = Z_{t-1} + \alpha(Z_{t-1} - Z_{t-2}) + X_t$$

so that a fraction α of last period's growth can be extrapolated, it follows that

$$Z_t = X_t + (1 + \alpha)X_{t-1} + (1 + \alpha + \alpha^2)X_{t-2} + \ldots + (1 + \alpha + \alpha^2 + \ldots + \alpha^t)X_o$$

and the outcome will still be a lognormal distribution. If $\alpha > 0$, so that rapid growth in period $(t - 1)$ makes rapid growth in period t more likely rather than less (and this is the likely direction of this correlation) then concentration will increase still more quickly. A combination of these two models has some appeal: rapid growth is liable to imply subsequent rapid growth, but large size signals relatively slow growth. If these relationships are of the simple linear kind we have postulated, then increasing aggregate concentration will be the overall outcome.

But an assumption which cannot easily be relaxed remains: that the second (and higher) moments of the distribution of growth rates are the same for all firms. One would expect the variance of growth rates to be lower for large firms than for small. It is much less likely for a large firm than for a small one that its fortunes will be transformed by a single spectacular success or failure. It is improbable that the results of the many activities which comprise the typical large firm will be perfectly correlated with each other, and the greater the number of activities the more improbable it is – in essence the assumption denies the possibility of effective diversification. We might consider this argument in a rather more formal way by supposing that firms consist of a number of independent activities, and the law of proportionate effect applies to each of these activities taken separately, so that the magnitude of individual activities will tend to be lognormally distributed. The size of particular firms is then obtained by summing variable numbers of these independent activities. But here problems begin. It is true that the *sum* of a random number of *normally* distributed variables is normally distributed (Feller 1966), and that the *product* of a random number of *lognormally* distributed variables is lognormally distributed: but the *sum* of a random number of *lognormally* distributed variables is neither normally nor lognormally distributed. Thus one cannot expect the outcome of this process, which is the most realistic description so far, to generate an approximation to any standard statistical distribution.

Merger cannot easily be fitted into the models we have been discussing, but in view of our findings that merger is the principal cause of changes in industrial structure it is important to see how this might be done. One of the few studies to consider this issue is that of Ijiri and Simon (1971), who suggest that observed departures from the Pareto curve may be attributable to the effect of mergers. In fact it seems to us more likely that the reverse is the case, and that to the extent that the Law of Proportionate Effect does in practice appear to hold, it is the influence of mergers which is largely responsible. The argument which underlies this is as follows. If there were no mergers, the greater diversification of activities which is characteristic of large firms would lead them to show a lower degree of dispersion of growth rates. To explore this, we have compared the distribution of growth rates of the 50 largest surviving firms of 1957 with a matched control group of 50 small firms (with 1957 assets between £1m and £2m). If we examine the 'internal' growth rates, i.e. those which we estimate would have occurred in the absence of merger, the variance of the large firms' experience is significantly lower at the 1 % level and the comparison of Lorenz curves in Table 7.1 shows that on any measure of inequality that distribution is the more concentrated. (There is some bias in this test, since the assumption of equal growth of both components of a merger leads to underestimation of the variance of the demerged growth rates, and more of our large firms engage in merger. We cannot quantify this effect, but doubt if its influence on the results is significant.) For external growth, by contrast, the assumptions of the Gibrat model are not implausible, since the size of acquisition which it is feasible for a firm to undertake is closely related to the existing size of that firm. While merger is not necessarily the principal cause, on average, of the magnitude of the growth of firms, it is almost always the principal contributor to the variance of the growth of firms, since merger is behind most cases of outstandingly rapid growth. As a result when we examine higher moments of the distribution of firms' growth rates it is the effect of mergers rather than internal growth which

TABLE 7.1. The inequality of business success

Cumulative % of all firms	Cumulative % of all growth			
	Internal		Total	
	Small firms	Large firms	Small firms	Large firms
10%	1·2%	4·8%	1·1%	3·8%
20%	5·7%	10·8%	5·2%	9·0%
30%	12·2%	17·8%	11·4%	15·2%
40%	19·7%	25·8%	18·6%	22·2%
50%	28·0%	34·5%	26·9%	29·8%
60%	38·0%	44·3%	36·6%	38·5%
70%	49·1%	55·1%	47·2%	48·1%
80%	61·1%	66·7%	59·3%	60·1%
90%	75·4%	80·5%	75·4%	75·6%

dominates, and so we observe little difference in the degree of dispersion of the growth rates of small firms and large. This is confirmed by our 1957–69 data. If we restore mergers and compare the actual distribution of growth rates, it is much harder to discriminate between them, as Table 7.1 shows. It therefore seems probable that one of the effects of a substantial reduction in merger activity would be a reduction in the validity of the lognormal or Pareto approximation to the observed distribution of the sizes of firms.

Of course, these models do not prove that concentration must always increase in the real world. We cannot deduce empirical propositions of this kind from *a priori* reasoning, and the assumptions which form the basis of those we deal with here are not susceptible to direct verification: while the power of central limit theorems is such that it would be unwise to claim support for any particular model from the observed characteristics of size distributions. Although log linear regression will not be enough to offset the tendency for concentration to rise, this form is the easiest to analyse rather than the most plausible to assume. But the models described do show that increasing concentration can occur in a wider range of circumstances than intuition would lead us to expect, and that it is even consistent with a mild but systematic tendency for large firms to suffer erosion of their markets by their smaller competitors.

THE GIBRAT EFFECT

We use the term 'Gibrat effect' to refer to a proposition that does not involve any of the heroic assumptions underlying the Law of Proportionate Effect. It rests on the argument of Chapter 4 above, and states simply that, if there is some dispersion in the growth rates of firms, concentration will tend to rise over time. This will be true even if there are no mergers and no tendency for large firms to grow more rapidly than small. If a group of rich men and a group of poor men visit Monte Carlo, it is likely that some of the rich will become poor and some of the poor rich: but it is also probable that some of the rich will get richer and some of the poor poorer, so that the extent of inequality within each group and over the two groups taken together is likely to increase. The process works to increase industrial concentration in precisely the same way, and we refer the reader back to Chapter 1 for a demonstration.

The direction of the effect is clear. What we must assess is its quantitative significance. It has been suggested by Hart and Prais (1956) that it accounted for the bulk of the increase in concentration before 1950. Our analysis above suggests that this is erroneous: but it is clear that some writers believe that the Gibrat effect is a major factor underlying the increases in concentration which we observe (Prais 1974). If this is so, there is little that can be done to prevent a secular upward trend in the degree of concentration, unless there is a very marked tendency as there was in Britain in the 1930s and 1940s for large firms to grow more slowly on average. Nor would it be particularly desirable to prevent an upward trend from such a source. In our Monte Carlo analogy, the extent to which dispersion increases depends on the size of the stakes involved in the game: in industrial structure, the extent to which dispersion increases also depends on the size of the stakes – the efficiency with which the economic system rewards success and penalises failure. While Monte Carlo confers rewards and penalties on the deserving and undeserving alike, it is unlikely that this is true in the same way of the economic system.

Thus there are two questions to be considered in an empirical analysis of the Gibrat effect. Firstly, how susceptible to change is the rank ordering of firms in the modern economy? We might reasonably take one view of the significance of high levels of concentration in the modern economy if the composition of the group of leading firms was constantly changing as they are challenged by vigorous newcomers: and a rather different view if these leaders could expect easily to maintain stability in their leading positions. Secondly, what is the likely size of the effect as a factor contributing to concentration increase in the U.K? We deal with each of these issues in turn below: but note here that if both these processes are of major significance we must conclude that competition and a wide dispersion of economic power are not in the long run compatible.

STABILITY AMONG THE INDUSTRIAL LEADERS

The simplest way of approaching this question is shown in Table 7.2, which shows the fate of the 100 largest manufacturing firms in the half century between 1919 and 1969. In each of the four sub-periods, the largest 100 firms were selected from the wider populations described in

TABLE 7.2. The fate of the leading 100 firms, 1919–69

	Surviving in top 100	Acquired by firm remaining in top 100	Dropout to lower rank
Status of top 100 firms of 1919 in 1930	52	17	31
Status of top 100 firms of 1930 in 1948	71	5	24
Status of top 100 firms of 1948 in 1957	71	3	26
Status of top 100 firms of 1957 in 1969	68	22	10

Chapters 5 and 6. We made our selection in such a way as to ensure that all entry to or exit from our top hundred represented genuine change, avoiding problems of comparability which have beset earlier work: thus, as Whittington (1972) acknowledges, his analysis exaggerates the turnover of large firms because many 'dropouts' are simply acquired by agencies outside the population (such as the government) and some 'newcomers' had done no more than gain market quotations.

However two problems of interpretation remain. Up to 1948 we used market value as a measure of firm size: from 1957 we use net assets. This means that there may be some artificial boost to turnover over the period 1948–57, when firms that may have (permanently) high valuation ratios will fall in rank ordering and those with lower market values relative to their assets will fall. But both are measures of capital employed and inspection of individual cases suggests that this is not a major distortion. It is also true that market value is a more volatile indicator than assets, as a result of the fickleness of stock market fashion on the one hand and the conservatism of accountants on the other, but this is by no means as serious a problem over our relatively lengthy periods as it is in the short run: however, the decline in mobility may be somewhat exaggerated on this account.

A second difficulty is that many of the largest firms drop out not because of any decline in relative size, but because they have been acquired by a firm which remains in the top 100; and this tendency is especially strong in the two periods of intensive merger activity. The treatment of such disappearances opens up considerable problems of interpretation. In some cases the acquired firm was a slow-growing firm which would in any case have been a dropout from the top 100, but in others – such as that of English Electric (acquired by G.E.C. in 1968) – there is no doubt that, had they remained independent, they would have remained among the leaders. Since there is no ideal way of treating these disparate cases (and their disparate effects on the chances of lower ranking firms remaining in the top 100), the problem is bypassed by recording disappearances by merger separately from the straightforward dropouts. (Since the incidence of merger is rather similar in

1919–30 and 1957–69 these periods can more easily be compared with each other than either of them can with the middle periods.) The general trend to increased stability is unaffected by either extreme assumption – that all acquired firms would, or would not, have remained within the top 100.

In 1919–30 only about half of all large firms survive, and their survival rate seems to be typical of large firms in the pre-corporate era. It is paralleled, for example, by the low survival rate of the top 50 firms of 1905 in 1919 (compare Payne 1967 with Hannah 1976, pp. 118–9), and it accords with Marshall's celebrated comparison of firms with trees of the forest: with the large ones doomed in the fullness of time to die (Marshall 1891). In all three periods after 1930, however, more than two-thirds of the firms survive and in the latest period since 1957 only 10% are straightforward dropouts. Moreover there is also increasing stability in the upper ranges of the distribution, which is not reflected in the table. In the earlier periods a few very large firms regularly dropped right out of the top 100 because of a decline in their relative size – Hadfields and Cammell Laird in 1919–30, Bovril and Hoare & Co. in 1930–48 – but the most marked declines of any of the top 50 firms in 1957–68 are those of Vickers (from 8 to 44) and Babcock and Wilcox (from 38 to 83). (It is interesting that these two firms are the best known instances of institutional pressure for managerial changes.) Almost all the dropouts in the modern period were ranked 81–100 in 1957 so that the dropout rate is no longer a reflection of dramatic declines in the relative size of one-time leaders. Most startling of all perhaps, as noted in Chapter 1, is that the six members of the 1957 'top ten' which survive to 1969 were all also in the 'top ten' in 1930.

These findings provide some confirmation of the view (Hannah 1976) that by the early 1930s the transition to a modern corporate economy had been achieved. They are also paralleled by the experience of the United States, where there was considerable downward size mobility among giant firms until the early 1920s, followed by a period of stability (Edwards 1975). It is generally recognised that the growth of large firms and the establishment of the corporate economy came somewhat earlier in the United States than in Britain (Hannah (ed.) 1976), and so the American precedence in increasing corporate stability is not unexpected. The underlying reasons for the growing stability of large corporations in the two economies are no doubt similar. Some are market leaders with entrenched oligopoly positions, so that it has been very difficult for newcomers to dislodge them. More recently in both countries large corporations (especially those in stagnant markets) have increasingly diversified their output so that they are now less dependent on demand conditions in any one market for their continued growth. At the same time the managerial techniques of managing large scale enterprises are now more widely diffused than was the case at an earlier stage of corporate development (Chandler 1962; Channon 1973 and cf. Payne 1967).

THE SIZE OF THE GIBRAT EFFECT

We cannot measure directly the impact which this Gibrat effect has had on concentration. *Ex post* we can observe the actual growth rate which a firm has enjoyed: but there is no way in which we can divide that growth into components which are and those which are not related to its initial size. *Ex ante* we might specify the growth which the firm was likely to experience in probabilistic terms. We could then compute the expected effect of this process on concentration, and compare it with the effect of all firms growing at their mean growth rates: so that we could separate out the impact of different growth expectations for firms of different sizes from the impact of deviations from these expected growth rates in particular cases. But we do not have such an *ex ante* probability distribution. What we have therefore sought to do is to estimate the significance of the Gibrat effect by combining these two approaches, regarding the *ex post* frequency distribution of growth rates for firms as a whole as an *ex ante* probability distribution of growth rates for each individual firm. What we are doing is to shuffle the pack of observed growth rates, so as to destroy any systematic relationship which may exist between size and growth rate by allocating randomly to each firm the growth rate experienced by another firm. In this way we can estimate separately the effect on concentration of that particular set of growth rates and of the particular order in which they are arranged.

Suppose the vector of the initial shares of firms is $\{S_i\}$, and they will end the period with shares $\{S_{ij}\}$ with probability P_j, then the expected value of the terminal value of our concentration index is

$$N_1 = \left(\sum_j \sum_i S_{ij}{}^\alpha P_j\right)^{\frac{1}{1-\alpha}} = \left(\sum_i S_i{}^\alpha \sum_j \left(\frac{S_{ij}}{S_i}\right)^\alpha P_j\right)^{\frac{1}{1-\alpha}}$$

Thus we must establish for each firm i the expected value of the expression $\left(\dfrac{S_{ij}}{S_i}\right)^\alpha$. We may estimate this using the observed distribution of growth rates g for all firms. (The distribution of normalised expected growth rates is not quite the same as the distribution of expected changes in market share, but if interdependencies between firms are small and no single firm is very large relative to the total the difference is not important.) Thus we have

$$N_1 = N_o\left(\sum_j \bar{g}_j{}^\alpha P_j\right)^{\frac{1}{1-\alpha}}$$

where N_o is the initial value of the concentration index.

We can apply this technique in a test of the hypothesis of Hart and

Prais (1956) that the Gibrat effect was substantially responsible for the increase in concentration in the inter-war period. We derived a distribution of g from those firms in our population for the period 1919–30 which did not engage in identified merger activity during the period – a total of 393 firms. We then compared the effects of this distribution with the actual observed concentration change over the period. The results of this are shown in column 4 of Table 7.3.

TABLE 7.3. The size of the Gibrat effect, 1919–30

		Equivalent number of firms					
	1	*2*	*3*	*4*	*5*	*6*	*7*
α	*Actual*	*Compromise*	*Actual*		*Alternative estimate:*		
	1919	*estimate,*	*1930*		*no. of observations*		
		1930		*393*	*391*	*385*	*376*
0·6	648	506	246	439	501	541	556
0·8	502	367	189	288	354	398	413
1·0	395	271	135	186	251	297	312
1·2	308	203	100	118	179	223	238
1·4	249	156	78	74	128	170	183
1·6	206	124	62	47	92	132	145
1·8	165	100	52	31	68	105	117
2·0	143	84	43	22	51	86	97

These figures are extremely high, especially for large α. Inspection of the underlying distribution readily provides an explanation. The mean growth rate over the period is 95 %: the standard deviation, however, is 463 %. Most of this variance is in fact attributable to a very small number of observations: by eliminating 2 of the 393 growth rates the variance is reduced by 75 %, and a further 6 reduce it by 90 %. All these extreme growth rates come from small firms: the largest, for example, is a firm with a 1919 valuation of £14,000. Although it was worth £977,000 by 1930, there were still over 200 firms larger. But even a 1 in 393 chance that J. & P. Coats (with a 1919 valuation of £45m giving it a 4·4 % share) will grow by a factor of 70 has a very substantial effect on our expectations of what will happen to concentration – especially for high α. But the probability that J. & P. Coats, or any similarly sized firm, will grow by a factor of 70 is not 1 in 393: it is nil. If Coats had grown by a factor of 70, it would by 1930 have been twice as large as the rest of manufacturing industry taken together!

This need not prevent us from using the observed distribution as a probability distribution: but it seems clear that it is necessary to use a truncated distribution, at least for large firms. We therefore re-estimated the figures in column 4 after the exclusion of some extreme observations. The results are shown in column 5 (which excludes 70-fold and 44-fold growth), column 6 (which limits growth to 10 times), and column 7 (which limits growth to 5 times). These restrictions are framed so that they maintain the hypothesis that the expected growth rate is the same for all firms in the distribution, but reduce the variance of the growth rates enjoyed by large firms.

Column 2 provides a reasonable 'compromise' estimate. It indicates the size of the Gibrat effect on the following assumptions.

    (i) all firms have the same expected growth rate

    (ii) the distribution of growth rates is that actually observed for non-merging firms but subject to the following restrictions

    (iii) the top ten firms cannot grow by a factor in excess of 5 (the fastest growing of these firms did in fact multiply its size by 5·7, largely by merger).

    (iv) no firm with 1919 valuation in excess of £5m can grow by a factor greater than 10 (the firm described in (iii) was the fastest growing firm in this category)

    (v) the two extreme observations (44 and 70), which are conceivable only for very small firms, are ignored.

We would judge that these figures certainly overstate the magnitude of the Gibrat effect. First, the restrictions specified in (iii)–(iv) above are probably too modest: we have probably under-estimated the extent to which size reduces the dispersion of expectations of growth. Second, there is surely *some* relationship between size and mean growth rate: because we have attributed all variation in growth rates to factors uncorrelated with size we have exaggerated the importance of these uncorrelated stochastic factors. Third, the measure of size we have used (market valuation) is likely to be the most volatile of all. Any other indicator would almost certainly exhibit smaller variance and so a smaller Gibrat effect.

In order to obtain some impression of the importance of the first two of these difficulties, we undertook some computer simulation experiments. For this we used our whole population of 1919 firms. The growth rate of each of these firms over the period 1919–30 was then determined by a random choice from our distribution of 393 growth rates. This process generated a hypothetical 1930 distribution of firms' sizes, in which any systematic relationship between the size or identity of a firm and its experience over the period has been destroyed. We undertook ten simulation runs of this kind. On one of them a large firm attracted one of the extreme observations described above, and as a result its 1930 market share was 47%. This simulation we discarded. We report these simulation results in Table 7.4, which shows that the results are satisfactorily consistent with the argument we have outlined above. The range is narrow and the average is close to the compromise estimate figures we derived in Table 7.3. The range is wider for high values of α (and relatively wider for low values of N in the CRN): this reflects the greater emphasis which high α places on the top part of the distribution

TABLE 7.4. Simulation estimates of the Gibrat effect, 1919–30

Indicator	Actual 1919	Nine accepted runs			Actual 1930
		Min.	Mean	Max.	
CR10	20·2%	20·3	24·5	27·4	38·0%
CR50	43·4%	47·0	50·9	53·9	63·7%
CR100	56·4%	61·5	64·6	67·5	77·4%
CR500	88·0%	91·8	92·4	93·2	99·6%
$\alpha = 1$	395	255	284	330	135
$\alpha = 2$	144	143	91	77	44

and the greater variance attaching to the average of a smaller number of relevant figures. The single negative figure is a reminder that, although the Gibrat effect will tend to increase concentration, it need not actually do so in every particular case. We have also considered the effect of the size–growth relationship by computing the average of $(\Sigma g^{\alpha})^{\frac{1}{\alpha-1}}$ for each of eight classes of firms grouped according to their 1919 size, so that the effect of variance between different size categories was reduced. This did not have significant effect on the estimates presented above.

TABLE 7.5. Simulation estimates of the Gibrat effect, 1957–69

Indicator	Actual 1957	Accepted runs			Actual 1969
		Min.	Mean	Max.	
CR10	24·6%	21·8	26·6	30·2	27·1%
CR50	48·4%	49·6	51·9	56·9	60·6%
CR100	60·1%	61·8	64·1	69·1	74·9%
CR500	88·9%	91·0	91·5	92·5	97·0%
$\alpha = 1$	324	233	280	317	187
$\alpha = 2$	92	71	99	119	71

For comparative purposes we have also used the simulation technique described above to estimate the significance of the Gibrat effect in the period 1957–69. The results of this experiment are displayed in Table 7.5. The pattern they show is generally consistent with our earlier analysis. The effect operates to generate significant concentration increases, but ones much smaller than those which did in fact occur in this period. The size of the effect also appears to be smaller than that which we observed for 1919 to 1930.

The nature of the Gibrat effect is such that it is not possible to observe the amount which it has contributed to concentration increase. What we have tried to do in the analysis presented here is to suggest a method of measuring the degree of variability in the growth rates of firms which enables us to see whether the rewards of success and the penalties of failure are sufficiently large to make the Gibrat effect a potentially significant factor in increasing concentration. Rather to our surprise, the answer to this question is 'yes'. It is not possible to conclude, as we had anticipated we might, that the effect is a curiosity of little practical significance. It seems that even if there were no merger and if large firms grew no faster than small, significant secular increases in concentration would still be observed. On the other hand, we can clearly reject the hypothesis that the principal cause of concentration increase has been the Gibrat effect. Our methods tend, if anything, to exaggerate its significance: but the analysis of our data shows that the impact of this factor on industrial concentration in the period was much smaller than the effect of merger.

8 Concentration and Public Policy

CONCENTRATION IN OTHER SECTORS

We have in this volume described the growth of concentration in private manufacturing industry in the U.K., and analysed its causes. This is not, of course, the only sector of the economy in which large organisations have substantially increased their role in the present century. The process of concentration through acquisition which we have seen at work in manufacturing had largely run its course in banking and in rail transport at an earlier date. The refining and distribution of oil products is dominated, here as elsewhere, by a handful of multinational oil companies. Construction is still the bastion of the small firm. The advantages of large scale production are slight, the flexibility of the small organisation is especially valuable: but here too concentration has been increasing substantially (Hillebrandt 1971).

In distribution the pioneers of innovative techniques in retailing have been able to achieve very rapid internal growth, and have turned small organisations into large firms in relatively short periods of time. Home and Colonial Stores, Burton and Woolworth were conspicuous in the inter-war period: but as our analysis in Chapter 3 would predict, each of these was slow to adapt to changing postwar conditions, and they were overshadowed by rapidly expanding competitors like Marks and Spencers and Tesco. Again in the 1970s innovation in retailing is arising not from the established giants but from outside, and explosive growth and the potential for future market leadership is seen in small firms like Asda and Comet. The role of merger in these developments has been very small: growth has been achieved by success in the marketplace, and expansion of capacity has been generated internally. Evidence on concentration increase in the retail sector is somewhat fragmentary (Bolton Committee 1971), but it suggests that, although the role of the very small establishment (turnover less than £10,000 p.a.) has diminished sharply, there is no unambiguous evidence of significant concentration increase. We should not be too quick to draw connections from structure to performance, but it is difficult to dispute that the performance of British retailing has been, by international standards, rather more effective than that of manufacturing.

TABLE 8.1. Government expenditure as a proportion of GNP, 1890–74

Year	Government expenditure (£m)	GNP (£m)	Expenditure as % of GNP
1890	131	1,472	8·9
1910	272	2,143	12·7
1930	1,145	4,386	26·1
1950	4,539	11,636	39·0
1960	8,350	22,875	36·5
1970	19,800	43,809	45·2
1974	36,468	73,977	49·3

Sources: Peacock and Wiseman (1961), Central Statistical Office (1975b)

TABLE 8.2. Government employment, 1911–73

Year	Armed forces	Civilian central government	Post Office and public corporations	Local government	Total government	Working population	Government as % of population
1911	343	115	155	660	1273	18509	6·9
1921	475	300	209	976	1960	19604	10·0
1931	360	244	197	1263	2064	21256	9·7
1950	690	827	2788	1419	5724	22982	24·9
1960	518	1303[a]	2200[a]	1737	5758	24526	23·5
1966	417	1405	1969	2134	5925	25583	23·2
1970	372	1537	2010	2411	6330	25124	25·2
1973	361	1608	1858	2714	6541	25005	26·2

(all figures in 000s)

Sources: Abramovitz and Eliasberg (1957), Department of Employment (1971), Department of Employment (1975).
  [a] There is a major reclassification between public corporations and central government between 1950 and 1960.

By far the most potent concentrating force outside manufacturing in Britain, and in other countries, has been the growth in the role of the State. Its effects in Britain have been especially great, since the system of government is highly centralised, with local authorities having few nominal powers and little real autonomy to exercise them. It has arisen from a number of sources: expansion in the supply of publicly provided services such as defence and education; increases in the government share of the market in areas, such as housing and transport, where it competes with non-government suppliers; and direct transfer of a range of functions to the government by nationalisation, as with health, coal and steel. The net result of these has been a very substantial rise in the proportion of resources disposed of by the state, and a less marked rise in the fraction of the working population employed by the government and government agencies (Tables 8.1, 8.2).

It is not our purpose here to engage in an assessment of the causes or consequences of these changes. The economic appraisal of concentration which we have attempted in Chapter 2 is of very little relevance to them, and a wide range of considerations are involved which we have not discussed here. But some of the characteristics of concentration which we described in Chapter 3 are found in, indeed epitomised by, the activities of the government. The formation of hierarchical structures, the loss of innovative capacity and flexibility in sets of formal rules, and the disappearance of a plurality of decision-makers, have been characteristic of the growth of the public sector. There have been compensating advantages. Most of the functions in which government agencies have expanded their role have been ones which the market performs badly: because they are such that the technical advantages of large-scale operation are overwhelming, as with electricity or telephones: because there are important social or economic aspects which private provision values inadequately, as with education and health: or because they are functions such as income maintenance and wealth redistribution which only the government can effectively provide.

Another area in which there has been substantial increase in concentration has been the growth of organised labour. Following some pioneering work by Hart and Phelps Brown (1957) we can analyse increases in trade union concentration in essentially the same way as we analyse increases in industrial concentration. The results are shown in Table 8.3. Since we include each non-unionised worker as a 'one-man union', the results are rather sensitive to the value of α chosen: at low α changes in the proportion of the workforce unionised have a major effect, while high α is principally concerned with the relative sizes of the largest unions. But, over the various time periods we have examined, the same trends are shown at all values of α. There are substantial increases in union concentration during both World Wars, but with a marked decline between 1919 and 1930 (the period of most rapid rise in *industrial* concentration) and a much smaller fall between 1948 and 1957. From 1902 to 1974 taken as a whole, there is a marked increase; and although it would be unwise to attach too much significance to this rather preliminary analysis, it is noticeable that there is some association between periods of rapid inflation and periods of increase in union concentration, a result foreshadowed by Hines (1964).

THE FUTURE OF CONCENTRATION

What is likely to happen to industrial concentration in the U.K. economy

TABLE 8.3. The growth of trade union concentration, 1902–74

Year	1902	1919	1930	1948	1957	1974
CR10	4·2%	15·0%	12·0%	22·0%	21·5%	27·4%
%age of workforce unionised	11·0%	40·3%	22·9%	41·8%	40·8%	46·4%
Numbers equivalent						
$\alpha = 0·6$	13,877,575	5,647,736	11,247,085	5,959,748	6,653,037	5,442,343
$\alpha = 0·8$	11,441,872	2,357,644	7,034,232	2,189,495	2,485,500	1,664,933
$\alpha = 1·0$	6,746,268	316,887	1,888,890	177,655	199,307	90,382
$\alpha = 1·2$	1,528,592	19,125	128,515	5,937	7,256	2,859
$\alpha = 1·4$	131,269	2,810	9,689	852	973	492
$\alpha = 1·6$	18,689	989	2,265	329	366	214
$\alpha = 1·8$	5,489	526	979	192	209	132
$\alpha = 2·0$	2,450	343	569	133	144	95
$\alpha = 2·5$	761	181	259	78	84	58
'Effective average' size						
$\alpha = 1·0$	2·7	62·1	11·2	126·2	120·9	280·0
$\alpha = 2·0$	7,486	57,405	37,200	168,601	167,319	265,582

Sources: Trades Union Congress (1902–75)

in the remainder of the twentieth century? In the absence of any marked change in public attitudes or policy, we can expect it to increase. The reason is simply that merger is the principal factor currently influencing industrial structure, and it is a factor which is asymmetric in effect. If merger activity is low, then it will increase concentration only slowly: if it is high, then it will increase it rapidly, but increase it it must. Only if the level of this activity is really very low, as it was in our 1930–48 period, is it conceivable that small firms can achieve sufficiently more rapid growth to offset these effects; but in all recent experience the number of acquisitions has much exceeded that level. However it makes very little sense to essay numerical conjectures about future concentration increases. If there is another merger wave comparable to that of the 1920s or 1960s, then apparently fanciful predictions (such as those of Newbould and Jackson 1972) of a hundred firms controlling 70% or 80% of all manufacturing activity could be fulfilled within ten or fifteen years. If there is no such craze – and current disenchantment with the results of recent mergers is at any rate sufficient to suggest that this is not immediately likely, though we expect some recovery from the recent very low levels – then such degrees of concentration may not be reached until the next century.

But we believe it is important to stress that we have a choice: that these developments are not inevitable. While it is certainly true that the optimal size of firm has risen in the last fifty years, we think there is reason to believe that the actual size of firms has risen to a much greater extent than this would justify. Certainly our analysis suggests that those small firms which have remained independent have had little difficulty in holding their own with their larger competitors. We are not, in this discussion, talking about very small firms. The smaller firms in our population would not qualify as 'small firms' under the Bolton Committee definition of having less than 200 employees. But they are still, by the standards of the industrial giants, mere minnows. In our 1969 population, for example, only 500 firms are ranked larger than Border Breweries of Wrexham, whose turnover was less than £5m and which employed fewer than 500 workers. Rapid growth in industrial concentration is not the unavoidable consequence of technological change, nor is it the product of an ineluctable Gibrat effect. (cf. Prais 1974) It arises from the very public – and if we wish preventable – process of merger. Since it is a good deal easier to stop concentration rising than to reverse such a trend once it has occurred, if we have doubts about its desirability there is a good deal of justification for erring on the side of restraint. What this would mean in practice would be a much tougher anti-merger policy, and we therefore devote the remaining part of our final chapter to a more detailed appraisal of the costs and benefits of such an approach.

MERGERS AND PUBLIC POLICY

In the U.S.A., where aggregate concentration is lower than in Britain, it is an established policy that merger which increases concentration in already concentrated markets should be prohibited. Since 1965 the British government has had power to control mergers which are thought to be against the public interest. Any merger in which the market share of the merging firms exceeds one-third (25% since 1973) or in which the gross assets to be acquired exceed £5m can be referred to the Monopolies Commission and, following an adverse finding, can be prohibited. Between 1965 and 1973, the government Mergers Panel examined about 800 mergers which *prima facie* met these criteria. 20 were referred to the Commission, of which 7 were abandoned voluntarily: of the remainder 7 were found not to be against the public interest, while 6 were not allowed to proceed (Gribbin 1974). In one of these cases (Ross Group and Associated Fisheries) the fishing interests were subsequently merged under the auspices of the government sponsored Industrial Reorganisation Corporation. Thus the legislation has operated to prevent the merger of the U.D.S. with Montague Burton, Lloyds with

Barclays and Martins, Rank with de la Rue, British Sidac with Transparent Paper, Boots or Beechams with Glaxo. Between the end of 1973 and the second quarter of 1976 the Office of Fair Trading has been more active, referring 17 mergers to the Monopolies Commission. Of these only three – Davy/British Rollmakers, Boots/House of Fraser and Herbert Morris/Amalgamated Industrials – have not been allowed to proceed. Indirectly the legislation may have deterred some mergers where the potential promoters were quite clear that they were acting against the public interest and that they would not be allowed to proceed – but such a low rate of prohibition is unlikely to have led such men to conclude that it was not worth taking a chance, and we may perhaps ignore the possibility.

It is possible to interpret these figures, as one government minister (Crosland, in B.o.T. 1969) has done, as implying that the gigantic wave of mergers in 1965–9 was almost universally beneficent in its impact, but we are more inclined to regard it as an indication that the policy has had negligible economic effect. Since we suspect that the public interest is promoted in rather less than 99% of all mergers, the issue of the adequacy of the existing law and the possibility of more stringent control is naturally raised. The principal element in such a policy would clearly be the abandonment of a case-by-case approach from a presumption of neutrality. This present *ad hoc* approach cannot be an effective mechanism for controlling merger and concentration because the investigative capacity required to monitor in detail thousands of merger proposals does not, and clearly cannot, exist. Nor would it be very useful even if it were feasible since many of the effects of concentration are effects of the process as a whole, and only to a very limited extent evident in any particular instance of it. Thus we have argued that increasing concentration has had major effects on the political relationship between government and industry – but the impact of any individual merger on this is negligible, and it would clearly be ludicrous to introduce such factors into an *ad hoc* appraisal. The erosion of the competitive environment which results from the merger of two small firms is insignificant, but the cumulative effect of many such mergers is not. It is impossible to identify anyone who is injured by the exhaust fumes from my car, and an investigation conducted in the style of the Monopolies Commission would quite properly conclude that no specific injury had been or was likely to be caused. Nevertheless it is certain that the effect of the exhaust fumes generated by motorists in general is detrimental to health, and generalised restriction is the appropriate remedy.

Thus the contrast between the British and American approaches to antitrust policy generally and to merger policy in particular is not (as many British commentators would wish to believe e.g. Howe 1971) a contrast between a pragmatic and a dogmatic approach, but between an ineffective and an effective approach. This is well understood in the

U.S. – Mason has commented that 'the demand for a full investigation of the consequences of a market situation or a course of business conduct is a demand for non-enforcement of the antitrust laws' (Mason 1957, p. 398). The choice which faces us is between a situation in which mergers are only exceptionally prohibited and one in which they are only exceptionally permitted. Intermediate possibilities are those in which the decision depends on some necessarily arbitrary rules of thumb – as with U.S. merger guidelines, intended to prevent large horizontal mergers and to allow others. The Utopian ideal of allowing desirable mergers and banning undesirable ones is not on the agenda of any serious discussion.

The relatively effective arm of British antitrust policy has been the Restrictive Practices Court – it is notable that Scherer (1970) in reviewing international antitrust policies discusses only the Court, the Commission not even rating a mention. The notion of adopting a similar approach to merger policy is appealing. This legislation imposes a general prohibition on cartel organisation, tempered by a series of 'gateways' for those which can show real social benefits in the face of a presumption that such activity is harmful. The early years of the Court's operations demonstrated that few agreements stood much chance of passing these tests (though there were some bizarre exceptions) and most firms abandoned the attempt to justify their restrictive practices. This legislative structure has been, by general standards of government intervention in industry, both cheap and effective (Elliott and Gribbin 1975). These characteristics, with the relative clarity of the nature of the procedure and the criteria to be applied, have led to the paradox that although the constraints which the restrictive practices legislation imposes on business behaviour are more stringent than those of the Monopolies Acts, the Court's activities appear to be viewed rather more favourably by the business community (Industrial Policy Group 1971a).

There would, however, be considerable difficulties in applying such a procedure, with clearly defined gateways, to merger policy. The Restrictive Practices Court has normally had the past behaviour of the industry before it as a guide to the reality of the benefits of the activities being defended: in the case of mergers, such benefits would accrue from prospective actions, and the Court's experience suggests that the effects on the public interest of unknown future events do not provide a readily justiciable issue. U.S. antitrust authorities have suffered from these difficulties – thus in 1958 the Bethlehem Steel Company argued that they could not build a large-scale steel plant in Chicago unless they were allowed to acquire a local company, but when the merger was prohibited they did construct such a plant. Specious predictions and empty threats are likely to be advanced, and there seems every reason to believe that they will win readier acceptance in the U.K. than the U.S. A further major problem is that a defence of economies of scale can be much more plausibly advanced in favour of merger than in support of a cartel. For these reasons we would expect many more cases to pass through 'gateways' in a British anti-merger policy. The costs of investigation would be higher, and the application criteria would be more complex. Further the timing of investigation would pose problems – it is possible to allow a restrictive practice to persist for some time before scrutiny can commence and while it is undertaken, but merger proposals require quick decisions and tend to be bunched in their incidence as they reflect transitory waves of enthusiasm or levels of share prices.

If, as we believe, the choice is between fairly extreme policies it is necessary to approach a change from the *status quo* with considerable circumspection. There are certain to be some losses from a vigorous anti-merger policy, and we shall look at them under three headings – scale economies, dynamic benefits associated with the growth of firms and the discipline on company managements provided by the threat of takeover. How severe are these reservations? The existence of economies of scale is the most frequently quoted justification for merger. There can be no doubt that there are a number of major industries in which such economies are of major significance, as a series of studies by the Cambridge Department of Applied Economics (Pratten and Dean 1965; Pratten 1971; Silberston 1971) have shown. The minimum efficient output of a modern oil refinery is such that to serve a British regional market by four or five refineries, rather than by two or three, would raise costs by more than a quarter. In the manufacture of nylon polymer, substantial cost increases would occur if there were more than three U.K. producers: while an airframe manufacturer selling only to the British market would face rapid competitive extinction, unless he gained substantial export markets to enable him to reach the greater scale and lower costs of his American competitors. While these industries are not representative of the economy as a whole, it is likely that their number is increasing. Although it is not easy to think of *a priori* reasons why technical progress should tend to increase the minimum efficient plant size, the belief that it does is widespread and it is certainly true that the cases mentioned above are all relatively 'new' industries.

There is, however, some reason to suppose that the gains from increased scale can be exaggerated, and the undoubted existence of economies of large size in some instances have been used very loosely by managements to justify mergers where such benefits have been claimed on the most dubious of grounds. In approving the merger of razor blade manufacturer Wilkinson Sword with British Match, the Monopolies Commission reported that 'we were told that "substance" included knowledge in depth of the cultural, political, financial and commercial aspects of a particular country; manufacturing experience (not necessarily of the product to be promoted); experience of local participation in management and in labour relations; time spent in acquiring such knowledge and experience, and reputation derived from commercial success. The benefits which Wilkinson could expect to receive from B.M.C. "substance" were, therefore, fundamental; nor were such benefits dependent upon sharing marketing systems or distribution channels although the possibility of such sharing would be explored. The companies were in agreement that, especially in marginal cases, the presence of enough "substance" to bear the weight of expansion or diversification was easier to recognise than to define.' (Monopolies Commission 1973, para. 46). And when Allied Breweries proposed merger with Unilever (both among Britain's ten largest companies) in the climax of the 1968 merger wave 'Both companies believed that Allied would derive substantial benefit from access to the services of Unilever's market research subsidiary, R.B.L. Since R.B.L.'s services can be bought by companies outside the Unilever group, they would, to the extent that Allied could pay for them, be available to Allied even if no merger took place; furthermore they would be unlikely to be available to any greater extent in the event of merger since they would still have to be paid for. However Unilever considered that, because of the closer relationship of companies within the group and the greater opportunities for continuous consultation, Allied would derive greater benefit from R.B.L.'s services in the event of the merger taking place.' (Monopolies Commission 1969, para. 92). It is never easy to determine whether the proponents of such vacuous arguments are attempting to deceive the Monopolies Commission or are simply, but more seriously, deceiving themselves.

Both these mergers were approved by the Commission: but the investigations were rather too much for the Industrial Policy Group (a group of leading businessmen) who protested that 'too much attention is given to detailed studies of the probable effects of the merger on economies of production, profitability, exports, balance of payments and managerial efficiency – all matters about which the parties directly concerned can, at that stage, only have rough ideas and hunches and can provide answers to the Board or the Monopolies Commission which neither is well equipped to judge of or to challenge.' (Industrial Policy Group 1971b, p. 13). It is difficult to reconcile this with the same group's claim that it is 'a caricature of things to suggest that any significant number of mergers of importance are formed in which operating efficiency and the return on capital are not the primary aims. The Board of Directors itself, especially of an acquiring company, may well be sceptical of schemes not closely enough linked to a profit and loss account. Shareholders, provided as they now are with more and more reliable information about past and probable future performances, have to be convinced about returns on investment.' (Industrial Policy Group 1971b, p. 10).

We are inclined to share the I.P.G.'s scepticism about the possibility of discriminating successfully between real and bogus claims to scale economies, and to believe that 'rough ideas and hunches' are the more accurate description of the normal situation. But we think that the prospect that a stringent anti-merger policy will prevent real economies being realised is slight. If they exist, then large firms will have lower costs than small and will be well able to expand their market share through internal growth. This has been characteristic of the motorcar industry, where the optimal output of a family saloon range is large relative to any (non-American) national market (Pratten 1971), but where successful producers have principally grown internally and merger, which by itself yields neither a plant of efficient size nor an increased demand for any specific model, does not appear to be an effective route to viability. More generally, merger may be a quicker route to optimal size, but internal growth is equally likely to lead to its realisation. The principal exception to this occurs where this optimal size is large relative to the size of any existing firm. In such cases it is possible that all domestic producers are at a disadvantage relative to foreign firms of the required size, or that no sub-optimal producer has a significant advantage over his equally sub-optimal competitors. There are certainly instances of this – the dominant producers in the U.K. computer and aircraft industries were formed by the amalgamation of small producers (though not small firms) each of which had poor prospects of survival as independent units. In such cases merger is likely to be the only feasible mechanism by which the necessary scale can be attained.

Are there many cases where all existing firms are too small for the successful exploitation of economies of large size? Some evidence on this may be obtained by comparing the extent of firm concentration and plant concentration. Economies of scale will mainly (though not exclusively) arise at the plant level. If firm concentration is significantly in excess of plant concentration, there is a *prima facie* case for supposing that the industrial structure is already sufficiently concentrated to permit available scale economies to be achieved. Useful data on this has been compiled by George and Ward (1975), who have computed the ratio of the CR4 by firms and by plants for industries in Britain, France and West Germany: the amount by which this index exceeds one may be interpreted as a rough measure of the extent to which industrial concentration is redundant as far as plant economies of scale are concerned. The results are shown in Table 8.4, and the pattern they present is very clear. In fact, where direct comparison is possible, the degree of redundancy in the U.K. exceeds that in West Germany in 35 out of 38 cases and that in France in 35 out of 40 cases. This is one demonstration of a general finding. British firms tend to be substantially larger than their European counterparts while British plants are not. George and Ward show that the British firms entering the CR4 in their group of industries are on average more than twice as large as corresponding German enterprises. But plants in Britain are, if anything, smaller than their German counterparts (Scherer 1973; Pryor 1972;

TABLE 8.4. Plant and firm concentration ratios

Redundancy $\left(\dfrac{4\,firm\ CR}{4\ plant}\right)$	No. of industries		
	U.K.	France	W. Germany
> 3	12	2	2
2·0 –3·0	13	7	6
1·5 –2·0	9	11	2
1·25–1·5	6	10	13
1·0 –1·25	1	10	15
	41	40	38

Source: compiled from George and Ward (1975)

George and Ward 1975) and the former two authors suggest that British plants are not substantially smaller than in the U.S., especially when employment is used to measure size. In the light of this evidence we think it is extremely difficult to argue that the present degree of industrial concentration in the U.K. is in general inadequate to allow scale economies to be realised: and if British economic performance is inhibited in this way that of our principal competitors is even more seriously retarded. There will be particular cases where a decisive change in technology means that merger is required to achieve the necessary scale of operation. But we believe such cases are rare, and have in practice been outnumbered by merger in pursuit of some mythical 'substance'. It would not be surprising to find that managers have a systematic bias in their judgement in favour of believing that they are capable of running greatly enlarged organisations, and make an optimistic appraisal of the benefits which will accrue if they are enabled to do so.

We believe, however, that some less widely canvassed arguments for merger carry more weight, and in particular that economies of growth may be more important than economies of scale. One industrialist (Knight 1972) has argued that 'to say that growth creates a good climate in a firm, helping morale and recruitment does not go far enough. Experience would dictate the much stronger assertion that growth is essential to build up and retain a good management team' and similar views are expressed in Penrose (1959). The point is well made, but in general we think it is desirable that this need for growth should be directed into the task of securing a greater market share by better products or superior efficiency, rather than satisfied by external acquisition: and this is an important argument against merger. But, for firms which face a stagnant or declining total market, it points in a rather different direction. Here superior relative performance means no more than slower absolute decline, and a firm can only achieve growth by merging with others in the industry to concentrate the remaining output in the hands of the most effective managers, or by using merger to diversify outside the industry. It is likely that there are many mergers of this type. The frenzied merger activity which has long been characteristic of the British brewing industry (Vaizey 1958) may largely be attributable to the combination of slow growth in total demand and a restrictive system of licensing outlets which make it difficult to achieve growth by other means. There is some evidence associating increasing concentration with relatively declining demand (George 1967). Diversification through merger is also common, and there are some indications that conglomerate merger is often the result of firms seeking to extricate themselves from markets whose growth prospects are poor. Weston and Manshinghka (1971) found that the American conglomerates they studied had raised below average earnings to the average for industry as a whole during their period of development.

The implications of this for public policy are equivocal. It is not in the public interest that firms which are failing in one industry should try their hand in others, and it is desirable that management should be encouraged to pursue internal rather than external routes to growth, where these are available. But it seems to us likely that Imperial Tobacco's successful diversification into potato crisp manufacture not only increased the competitiveness of the crisp market (Bevan 1974) but also, through its effects on managerial morale, increased the efficiency of the tobacco industry. It is argued by Cyert and George (1969) that firms can and should be encouraged to pursue diversification from internal resources alone, but the success rate of firms which are required to build up capacity in an unfamiliar industry entirely from scratch is likely to be low, and the economic costs of both the unsuccessful ventures which result, and the potentially successful enterprises which are deterred, may be high. Management skills can be transferred to new industries by altering the employment of the managers rather than the function of the firm – in the nationalised sector there has been a substantial transfer of skilled managerial personnel from the (declining) National Coal Board to the (expanding) electricity supply authorities. But the management capacity of an organisation consists of more than the sum of the skills of its individual managers, and such transfers are likely to have further deleterious effects on the confidence of those who remain with the declining industry. There consequently seems to be a stronger case for *ad hoc* assessment of conglomerate merger than for others: and since such mergers are a relatively small proportion of the total (Kuehn (1975) estimated that less than 8 % of those he studied were conglomerate) this may be a practicable proposal.

A somewhat different argument arises from the common practice by which small firms develop new ideas, enjoy rapid growth and sell out to larger firms. Jewkes, Sawers and Stillerman (1958) have noted the ubiquity of this phenomenon, which they attribute to the difficulties which small firms face in raising the capital required for the successful exploitation of innovation. The Bolton Committee described a rather wide range of sources of such capital, but also observed that such firm disappearances were frequent – 13 % of small firms in manufacturing and construction in 1963 had been taken over by 1970. There can be little doubt that a major motivation in this process is the impact of the taxation system. In the U.K. (in 1975) earned income over £20,000 per annum is taxed at 83 % and investment income at 98 %. This puts pressure on the successful inventor or entrepreneur to turn his rewards into capital gains (taxed at a maximum of 30 %), and he can only do this by selling the business or a substantial part of it to the public or to another company. It is likely that blocking this loophole through anti-merger policy would be economically damaging: but the problem is one of taxation rather than antitrust policy, and it would be better to persuade governments to eschew tax rates of a magnitude which is only tolerable because they are ineffective, and allow the capital structure of a small business to be determined by its financial requirements.

Perhaps the most serious objection to a rigorous anti-merger policy is its effect of severely inhibiting the operation of the market for corporate control. The possibility of takeover is an important part of the mechanism by which the competitive system disciplines weak or unenterprising management, and deters those who control the firm from pursuing objectives which contribute more to their own utility than to the profitability of the company. Its operation is well described in general terms by Manne (1965) and in a particular instance by Pratten (1970). Pratten describes the fate of Greengate and Irwell Rubber. This company's approach is epitomised in its view that 'we believe it best to continue to apply ourselves to improving efficiency and developing products within our natural environment of knowledge and machinery, rather than explore where the grass may look greener, but which could be potential losers for those neither accustomed to nor understanding how to earn such apparently easy money' (an extract from the 1964 Chairman's report, cited by Pratten). In 1967 it was acquired by Slater Walker Securities, who reorganised the company and raised profits by 67 % within two years. They subsequently divested its principal activities to form the Allied Polymer Group, which for some time had a satisfactory record of growth and profitability. Such activity not only raises the efficiency of firms involved, but acts as a stimulus to efficiency in others – Pratten notes that B.T.R., another rubber goods producer with an even worse record than G. and I., reconstituted their management at about the same time and substantially increased their profitability. Though Slater Walker's actions are no longer viewed with the same enthusiasm and doubts are cast on the value of the management skills they brought to bear, there can be little doubt that for a period their existence provided a real deterrent to idle management. More conventionally the weak long-term performances of Courtaulds and A.E.I. were brought to an end by reorganisations subsequent to the bids by I.C.I. (unsuccessful) and G.E.C. (successful) respectively. The prospect of a similar fate for Vickers, made more real when the much smaller Williams Hudson Group built up and for a time maintained a threatening 23 % shareholding, was almost certainly an influence behind the managerial changes and subsequent rises in profitability in that company in the 1970s.

Thus we run rather counter to some recent opinion in finding more likelihood of benefit in conglomerate merger than in amalgamation within the same industry. It is easy to see how conglomerates have acquired their bad name. When the stock market attaches dizzy valuations to pieces of paper which represent no more than a share in the financial genius of a company promoter, the temptation for the promoter to exchange this paper for tangible assets through merger is strong: and when the market's faith in his genius wanes, it is everyone else who is left a little poorer. But the activities of Ling-Temco-Vought or Slater Walker Securities are exceptional and, given the effects of the threat which they posed to the security of managers making less than full use of the assets under their control, it is not at all clear that they were undesirable.

Despite this anecdotal evidence there have been recent attempts to deny the reality of the market in corporate control as a constraint on business behaviour by examination of the characteristics of larger samples of quoted firms (Singh 1975; Reddaway 1972). These writers have noted that, although low profitability does increase the probability of takeover, the relationship is not a very strong one: that in any particular year unprofitable firms are still more likely to remain independent than not: and that a number of highly profitable firms are acquired. Their arguments are not, however, convincing. If the threat of takeover were a completely effective deterrent to non-profit-maximising behaviour, we would expect to observe *no* relationship between profitability and probability of acquisition, since all firms would be making the maximum available profits and all mergers would occur for other reasons. If there are few convictions for arson, we should consider the possibility that not many people want to set houses on fire, or that the penalties deter them, before concluding that the skies are ablaze with the activities of unpunished arsonists. In fact the relationship between profitability* and the likelihood of takeover will be lower, the greater the

---

*Or more accurately the difference between actual and potential profitability, though the latter would be the same for all firms if asset valuations and profit measurements fully reflected the underlying economic concepts.

effectiveness of the deterrent, and the stronger the chance that the low profitability will be punished if it occurs. The actual correlation between the two will reflect the balance of these two factors, so that the observed relationship may reflect the fact that (a) the deterrent is ineffective and the threat has no reality and (b) the deterrent is very effective and so is the threat. Similar arguments apply to the valuation ratio, an indicator used by some other writers (Newbould 1970; Singh 1971; Kuehn 1975).

Thus statistical tests of that kind are necessarily inconclusive, and to appraise the impact of mergers under this heading and under those we have previously discussed it is more appropriate to examine the actual performance of merging firms. Newbould's interviews, though not particularly probing, found managers' assessments of the effects of mergers centred on the problems which had followed them and that the most frequently offered explanation of the reasons for merger was 'fashion' (Newbould 1970). Studies of the relationship between the total profitability of the merging firms and the subsequent record have shown that there is no positive effect on profitability and possibly a negative one (Singh 1971; Utton 1974). Hogarty (1970) has surveyed the American evidence, with similarly depressing conclusions. The kinds of analysis which an outsider can undertake are necessarily rather superficial, and it is possible that the gestation period for the benefits of merger is sufficiently long to make these profitability comparisons misleading: though longer run analyses of share price performance have suggested that it is, at best, not advantageous to be a shareholder in a firm engaging in substantial acquisition activity. It is possible that analysis of internal company data on costs and profits would show benefits of a kind which are not evident from published information. In the early 1970s the National Institute for Economic and Social Research, a respected independent research unit with substantial support from government and industry, approached a number of leading firms with a view to analysing the effects of recent mergers in this way. The degree of cooperation which they were offered was so low that they were forced to abandon the project.

If the benefits of merger were large, it is unlikely that evidence of them would be so elusive. We do not think that many benefits would be lost if merger were henceforth a rarer occurrence.

Appendix

Alternative Populations, Alternative Results?
Our results for 1919–30 and 1930–48 differ in some respects from those of
Hart and Prais published in their inaugural study of long-term trends in
aggregate concentration in the *Journal of the Royal Statistical Society*,
1956. Since their study has been widely quoted in the literature, we
provide here an analysis of the sources of our differences.

We have followed Hart and Prais in using the most readily accessible
data for this period as a measure of size: the market value of quoted
companies. It is easy to envisage *a priori* objections to this measure, (see
pp. 42–3 above), though we were pleasantly surprised when matching
changes in market valuation against more conventional measures such as
value added or gross output (which existed for some firms) to find them
reasonably closely related. The starting point for assembling our
population of firms in 1919, 1930 and 1948 was the *Stock Exchange Daily
Official List*. All firms which were engaged in domestic manufacturing
industry (as defined by orders III–XIX of the *Standard Industrial
Classification* for 1958) and which were listed on the London Stock
Exchange on 2 January 1919 and 31 December 1930, or on the latter date
and 31 December 1948, were included. A few provincially quoted firms
listed in the *Investors' Monthly Manual* were also added to the
population. Firms operating principally abroad with few U.K. assets and
firms engaged principally in mining or distribution were excluded,
(unless they were acquired by a manufacturing firm in the relevant
period). Market values were obtained from published data (*Stock
Exchange Daily Official Lists, Stock Exchange Year Books, Stock
Exchange Official Intelligences*) on issued capital and stock exchange
prices, except that where some capital was not quoted, and could not be
directly valued, we made approximations of the value of the unquoted
capital.

In our pilot study of 1919–30 it became obvious that many of the firms
which appeared in 1919 but not in 1930, were not genuine 'deaths' but
merely firms which lost their quotation; perhaps, for example, by being
acquired by a foreign parent. Similarly some 1930 firms which did not
appear in 1919 were thriving in 1919 but did not gain a quotation until
after that date: they were not new entrants in any meaningful sense.
Several large private firms were also known to have been excluded both
in 1919 and 1930. Accordingly values for these categories of excluded

firms were estimated for 1919 and/or 1930, using a variety of expedients aimed at approximating their market value as going concerns. Three main methods were used. If a firm was quoted (or sold for a known sum) at some stage after 1919, we converted its value at the time of quotation (or sale) to 1919 values by an appropriate industry share price index, adjusted where necessary by known facts about the dividend yield or the prior rate of growth of individual firms. We adopted a similar procedure to obtain a 1930 value for firms which lost quotations after 1919 but which still maintained an independent existence in 1930. Failing this expedient we obtained data on profits and dividends and derived an estimate on the basis of average price-earnings ratios and dividend yields. Finally for a very small number of privately controlled firms for which no financial information was available we estimated a 'market value' from data on market shares in relation to other firms in the same industry for which we did have value data. These additions and adjustments to the *Daily Official List* population could be made only where data was available. It would not have been possible to improve the coverage of our population further, except by using increasingly conjectural estimates in which we could have placed little confidence.

Our wider population for 1930–48 was constructed on precisely analogous principles, to maintain a constant population of firms at both dates.

The reader who compares this account with that of Hart and Prais will find that they examined changes in concentration in a population consisting of 571 quoted companies in 1907, 726 in 1924, 837 in 1939 and 2103 in 1950. Unfortunately the original matrices of the Hart–Prais study have not been preserved by the National Institute of Economic and Social Research which sponsored the study. However from reconstruction of published data it appears that the main differences between the studies are due to the following constrasts in approach:

1. Hart and Prais included a number of distribution and mining companies; we included only manufacturing companies.
2. We included some unquoted or provincially quoted companies; Hart and Prais included only London quoted companies.
3. Our populations have few births because they include the majority of large firms at all dates (whether or not they were quoted at the time). The rising number of firms in Hart–Prais reflects companies newly receiving a quotation rather than new entrants in the conventional sense. Our populations, by contrast, show a decline both in 1919–30 and in 1930–48 since there are few 'births' to offset 'deaths' by merger.

Our results differ from those of Hart and Prais in two major respects: in the index of concentration used and in the importance we attach to merger as a source of historical concentration increase. These two areas of difference are not unrelated for, as we have shown in Chapter 4, the index used by Hart–Prais – the variance of logs – is quite unsuitable as a measure of concentration. Fortunately, however, it did not falsify their results. They suggested that concentration rose both in 1907–24 and in 1924–39 but fell between 1939 and 1950. We have recalculated from their original data the changes in concentration of constant populations of firms using more reliable concentration indexes. Both the direction and the magnitude of changes are the same as those indicated by the variance of logs and reported by Hart–Prais (Hannah 1976, appendix 2). Their findings on changes in the *level* of concentration, though they use different dates, may be taken broadly to confirm our own; certainly their results are compatible with ours.

In other respects, however, the use of the variance of logs as an index of concentration can lead to serious errors. One illustration of this is that mergers appear to have been of small importance in 1919–30 in our own population when their impact is measured by the variance of logs – a clearly untenable result when seen in the light of the contrary results for the whole range of CRNs and αs in Figure 5.1. Indeed one of the perverse properties of the variance of logs is that, in some populations, the more mergers there are, the less they increase concentration!

However on further examination of the data, it became clear that the major difference between their findings and ours can be traced to the coverage of their merger data, rather than to the measure used. Professor Hart tells us that lack of time and resources prevented a fuller treatment of merger in their study, and their published account makes clear that only a small proportion of manufacturing mergers are captured by their method. They did, in fact, exclude more than 99% of all mergers, and more than 80% of all large mergers (Hannah 1972, pp. 193–202, 279–94). Some reconstruction of their merger population was possible from published data, and this suggested that the extensive omissions were inherent in the method of capturing mergers adopted in their study. To take a simple, but not untypical, case, a merger of four large firms in 1923, one of which had been quoted in 1907, would be registered by their method as an effect not of merger but as the internal growth of the 1907 quoted firm. Thus much of the increase in concentration within their population which they attributed to internal growth was, in fact, the result of merger. To avoid this error, when a firm in our population was known to have made a significant acquisition in 1919–30 or 1930–48, we added the acquired firm to our population in 1919 or 1930 so that its effect could be incorporated. Nonetheless our own study also suffers from excluding the majority of mergers. However we estimate that we have included more than 80% of the large mergers of the period so that the errors due to omissions have been limited.

We conclude then that our results more accurately reflect the importance of merger in this period than do those of Hart and Prais. We should also consider further the suggestion of Hart and Prais that the

Gibrat effect, rather than mergers, was the major cause of concentration increase before 1950. As we have shown in Chapter 7, there can be no serious doubt that the Gibrat effect was much less important than merger in increasing concentration between 1919 and 1930. The procedure adopted by Hart and Prais (and subsequently by Utton 1971) for this estimation is to undertake least squares estimation of the equation

$$Z_{t+1} = \alpha + \beta Z_t$$

where Z is the log of the size of the firm. The residual variance of Z_{t+1} subsequent to this estimation is then attributed to the impact of the Gibrat effect between periods t and $(t+1)$. Our procedure differs from this in essentially three ways (other than in choice of measure). We have not sought to estimate such a relationship between size of firm and growth rate, since we suspect that in the 1919–30 period (the only one in which such a relationship was of any significance as far as *internal* growth was concerned) it is a good deal more complex in form than this log-linear relation suggests. As a result our estimates of the Gibrat effect are biased upwards, though as noted (p. 108) we have assessed the likely effect of such bias and judge it to be small. On the other hand, we have established (p. 102) that a major part of the variance of firms' growth rates is attributable to merger, which typically affects different firms in very different ways, and we have removed the influence of this factor before undertaking our estimates. We have also taken steps to ensure that our results are not distorted by the behaviour of one or two small firms with exceptional experiences; and if our data is any guide this is potentially a factor of considerable importance. We are satisfied that the likely direction of the remaining bias in our estimates is upward.

We should also note that our results for 1957–69 differ substantially from those of Utton (1971) for the period 1954–65, and again we find the role of merger to be considerably greater. Our data relates to a somewhat different period, and the intensity of merger activity was much greater between 1966 and 1969 than in the mid-fifties, but we suspect that this is only a minor part of the discrepancy between his results and ours. We believe differences of technique are probably more important. Utton used variance of logs as concentration indicator. This deficiency was much aggravated by the fact that he also used data grouped in a rather unfortunate way, so that one-third of all firms fell into his smallest size category. This means that in a period in which all firms are growing it is much harder for a small firm to rise into a higher size category than for a large one. It is therefore highly probable that data so grouped will show an apparent increase in concentration whether such an increase occurs in reality or not, and we think it likely that Utton was misled by this into exaggerating the role of internal growth.

Bibliography

(Unless otherwise stated, the place of publication of books cited in this bibliography is London.)

Aaronovitch, S. and Sawyer, M.C. (1975), *Big Business*.

Abraham, N. (1974), *Big Business and Government*.

Abramovitz, M. and Eliasberg, V.F. (1957), *The Growth of Public Employment in Great Britain* (Princeton).

Acton Society Trust (1953, 1957) *Size and Morale*.

Adelman, M.A. (1951), 'The Measurement of Industrial Concentration', *Review of Economics and Statistics*.

Adelman, M.A. (1969), 'Comment on the "H" Concentration Measure as a Numbers Equivalent', *Review of Economics and Statistics*.

Aitchison, J. and Brown, J.A.C. (1954), 'On Criteria for Descriptions of Income Distribution', *Metroeconomica*.

Aitchison, J. and Brown, J.A.C. (1957), *The Lognormal Distribution* (Cambridge).

Alford, B.W.E. (1973), *W.D. & H.O.Wills and the Development of the U.K. Tobacco Industry, 1786–1965*.

Armstrong, A. and Silberston, A. (1965), 'Size of Plant, Size of Enterprise and Concentration in British Manufacturing Industry 1935–58', *Journal of the Royal Statistical Society* series A.

Arnold, T. (1939), address to Denver Bar Association, 15 May 1939, as quoted in Brady (1943), pp. 14–15.

Atkinson, A.B. (1970), 'On the Measurement of Inequality', *Journal of Economic Theory*.

Bagehot, W. (1867), *The English Constitution* (Page references to N. St. John Stevas (ed.), *Collected Works of Walter Bagehot*, Vol. V, 1974).

Bailey, D. (1973), 'The Determinants of Labour Turnover: A Cross-Sectional Study of British Manufacturing Industry', *University of East Anglia, Department of Economics Working Paper*.

Bain, G.S. (1970), *The Growth of White Collar Unionism* (Oxford).

Bain, J.S. (1951), 'Relation of Profit Rate to Industry Concentration: American Manufacturing, 1936–40', *Quarterly Journal of Economics*.

Bannock, G. (1971), *The Juggernauts: The Age of the Big Corporation*.

Bates, J. (1965), 'Alternative Measures of the Size of Firms', in P.E. Hart (ed.) *Studies in Profit, Business Saving and Investment in the United Kingdom, 1920–62*, vol. 1.

Berge, C. (1963), *Topological Spaces* (Edinburgh).

Bernstein, M. (1955), *Regulating Business by Independent Commission* (Princeton).

Bevan, A. (1974), 'The U.K. Potato Crisp Industry, 1960–72; A Study of New Entry Competition', *Journal of Industrial Economics.*

Blauner, R. (1960), 'Work Satisfaction and Industrial Trends in Modern Society', in W. Galenson and S.M. Lipset (eds.) *Labour and Trade Unionism: An Interdisciplinary Reader* (New York).

Board of Trade (1969), *Mergers: A Guide to Board of Trade Practice.*

Bolton Committee (1971), *Report of the Committee of Inquiry on Small Firms* (Chairman J.E. Bolton, Cmd 4811).

Booth, C. (1903), *Life and Labour of the People of London.*

Boyle, S.E. (1973), 'The Average Concentration Ratio: An Inappropriate Measure of Industry Structure', *Journal of Political Economy.*

Bracher, K.D. (1971), *The German Dictatorship: The Origin, Structure and Effects of National Socialism.*

Brady, R. (1933), *The Rationalization Movement in German Industry* (Berkeley).

Brady, R. (1943), *Business as a System of Power* (New York).

Brittan, S. (1964), *The Treasury Under the Tories.*

Business Monitor (various dates), M7, *Acquisitions and Mergers of Companies.*

Camra (Campaign for Real Ale) (1974), *Good Beer Guide* (ed. J. Hanscomb, Leeds).

Caves, R. E. (1968), 'Market Organisation, Performance and Public Policy', in Caves (ed.), *Britain's Economic Prospects.*

Central Statistical Office (1958), *Standard Industrial Classification.*

Central Statistical Office (1975a), *Input-Output Table for the U.K. (1971).*

Central Statistical Office (1975b), *National Income and Expenditure, 1964–74.*

Champernowne, D.G. (1953), 'A Model of Income Distribution', *Economic Journal.*

Chandler, A.D. (1962), *Strategy and Structure: Chapters in the History of Industrial Enterprise* (Cambridge, Mass.).

Channon, D.F. (1973), *The Strategy and Structure of British Enterprise.*

Child, J. (1969), *The Business Enterprise in Modern Industrial Society.*

Cleland, S. (1955), *The Influence of Plant Size on Industrial Relations* (Princeton).

Cole, G.D.H. (1918), *Self-Government in Industry.*

Coleman, D.C. (1969), *Courtaulds: An Economic and Social History*, vol. 2 (Oxford).

Collins, W.R. and Preston L.E. (1968), *Concentration and Price-cost Margins in Manufacturing Industries* (Berkeley).

Cowling, K.G. and Waterson, M. (1974), 'Price-cost Margins and Market Structure', *Warwick Economic Research Papers*, no. 44.

Cyert, R.M. and George, K.D. (1969), 'Competition, Growth and Efficiency', *Economic Journal*.

Dalton, H. (1920), 'The Measurement of the Inequality of Incomes', *Economic Journal*.

Davies, J.R. and Kelly, M. (1971), *Small Firms and the Manufacturing Sector*, Bolton Committee Research Report, no. 3.

Dasgupta, P., Sen, A. and Starrett, D. (1973), 'Notes on the Measurement of Inequality', *Journal of Economic Theory*.

De Jong, H.W. (1971), *Onderneningsconcentratie* (Leiden).

Dell, E. (1973), *Political Responsibility and Industry*.

Demsetz, H. (1973), 'Industry Structure, Market Rivalry and Public Policy', in J.F. Weston and S.I. Ornstein (eds.) *The Impact of Large Firms on the U.S. Economy* (Lexington).

Department of Employment (1971), *British Labour Statistics: Historical Abstract 1886–1968*.

Department of Employment (1975), *British Labour Statistics, 1973*.

Department of Employment (1976), 'The Incidence of Industrial Stoppages in the U.K.', *Department of Employment Gazette*, February.

Department of Trade and Industry (1973), *British Shipbuilding 1972; A Report to the DTI by Booz, Allen and Hamilton International*.

Dewey, D. (1961), 'Mergers and Cartels: Some Reservations about Policy', *American Economic Review*.

Downs, A. (1967), *Inside Bureaucracy* (Boston).

Eaton, B.C. and Lipsey, R.G. (1975), 'The Principle of Minimum Differentiation Reconsidered: Some New Developments in the Theory of Spatial Competition', *Review of Economic Studies*.

Edwards, R.C. (1975), 'Stages in Corporate Stability and the Risks of Corporate Failure,' *Journal of Economic History*.

Elliott, D.C. and Gribbin J.D. (1975) 'The Abolition of Cartels and Structural Change in the United Kingdom', paper read at the *Second International Conference on the Economics of Industrial Structure*, Nijenrode, Netherlands, 1975 (published 1976 eds., A.P. Jacquemin and H.W. de Jong).

Evely, R. and Little, I.M.D. (1960), *Concentration in British Industry*.

Feinstein, C.H. (1972), *National Income, Expenditure and Output of the United Kingdom, 1856–1965*.

Feller, W. (1966), *An Introduction to Probability Theory and its Applications*, vol. 1 (New York).

Financial Times (1976), *Industrial Ordinary Share Index, 1930–76*, (Financial Times Library, typescript).

Galbraith, J.K. (1967), *The New Industrial State*.

George, K.D. (1967), 'Changes in British Industrial Concentration 1951–8', *Journal of Industrial Economics*.

George, K.D. (1975), 'A Note on Changes in Industrial Concentration in the U.K.' *Economic Journal*.

George, K.D. and Ward T.S. (1975), *The Structure of Industry in the EEC* (Cambridge).

Gibrat, R. (1931), *Les Inégalités Économiques* (Paris), partly translated and reprinted as 'On Economic Inequalities', *International Economic Papers* (1957).

Goldthorpe, J.H. *et al.* (1970), *The Affluent Worker: Industrial Attitudes and Behaviour* (Cambridge).

Gowing, M. (1974), *Independence and Deterrence*.

Graham, A. (1972), 'Industrial Policy', in W. Beckerman (ed.) *The Labour Government's Economic Record: 1964–70*.

Grand Metropolitan (1975), Chairman's Statement, *Annual Report and Accounts*.

Gribbin, J.D. (1974), 'The Operation of the Mergers Panel since 1965', *Trade and Industry*, 17 January.

Hall, M. (1952), 'Monopoly Policy', in G.D.N. Worswick and P.H. Ady (eds.) *The British Economy 1945–50* (Oxford).

Hall, M. and Tideman, N. (1967), 'Measures of Concentration', *Journal of the American Statistical Association*.

Hall, M. and Weiss, L. (1967), 'Firm Size and Profitability', *Review of Economics and Statistics*.

Hannah, L. (1972), 'The Political Economy of Mergers in Manufacturing Industry in Britain between the Wars' (unpublished D.Phil. thesis, Oxford).

Hannah, L. (1974a), 'Mergers in British Manufacturing Industry, 1880–1918' *Oxford Economic Papers*.

Hannah, L. (1974b), 'Managerial Innovation and the Rise of the Large-scale Company in Interwar Britain', *Economic History Review*.

Hannah, L. (1976), *The Rise of the Corporate Economy*.

Hannah, L. (ed.) (1976), *Management Strategy and Business Development*.

Hardy, G.L., Littlewood, J.E. and Polya, G. (1934), *Inequalities* (Cambridge).

Hart, P.E. (1960), 'Business Concentration in the United Kingdom', *Journal of the Royal Statistical Society*, series A.

Hart, P.E. (1968), 'A Long Run Analysis of the Rate of Return on Capital in Manufacturing Industry, United Kingdom, 1920–62', in P.E. Hart (ed.) *Studies in Profit, Saving and Investment in the U.K., 1920–62*, vol. 2

Hart, P.E. (1971), 'Entropy and other Measures of Concentration', *Journal of the Royal Statistical Society*, series A.

Hart, P.E. and Phelps Brown, E.H. (1957), 'A Study in the Laws of Aggregation', *Economic Journal*.

Hart, P.E. and Prais, S.J. (1956), 'The Analysis of Business Concentration: a Statistical Approach', *Journal of the Royal Statistical Society*, series A.

Hart, P.E., Utton, M. and Walshe, G. (1973), *Mergers and Concentration in British Industry* (Cambridge).

Hayek, F. (1944), *The Road to Serfdom.*

Herfindahl, O.C. (1950), 'Concentration in the U.S. Steel Industry' (unpublished doctoral dissertation, Columbia).

Hicks, J. (1935), 'Annual Survey of Economic Theory – the Theory of Monopoly', *Econometrica.*

Hillebrandt, P.M. (1971), *Small Firms in the Construction Industry* Bolton Committee Research Report No. 10.

Hines, A.G. (1964), 'Trade Unions and Wage Inflation in the United Kingdom: 1893–1961', *Review of Economic Studies.*

Hirschman, A.O. (1964), 'The Paternity of an Index', *American Economic Review.*

Hogarty, T.F. (1970), 'Profits from Merger: the Evidence of 50 Years', *St. John's Law Review.*

Holland, S. (1975), *The Socialist Challenge.*

Holtermann, S.E. (1973), 'Market Structure and Economic Performance in U.K. Manufacturing Industry', *Journal of Industrial Economics.*

Hotelling, H. (1929), 'Stability in Competition', *Economic Journal.*

Howe, M. (1971), 'Anti-trust Policy: Rules or Discretionary Intervention', *Moorgate and Wall St.*

Hughes, J. (1972), 'The Trade Union Response to Mergers', in J.M. Samuels (ed.) *Readings on Mergers and Takeovers.*

Hunter, A. (1969), 'The Measurement of Monopoly Power', in A. Hunter (ed.) *Monopoly and Competition.*

Hutchinson, H. (1965), *Tariff Making and Industrial Reconstruction.*

Ijiri, Y. and Simon, H.A. (1971), 'Effects of Mergers and Acquisitions on Business Firm Concentration', *Journal of Political Economy.*

Indik, B.P. (1965), 'Organisational Size and Member Participation: Some Empirical Tests of Alternative Explanations', *Human Relations.*

Industrial Policy Group (1971a), *The Control of Monopoly.*

Industrial Policy Group (1971b), *Merger Policy.*

Ingham, G.K. (1970), *Size of Industrial Organisation and Worker Behaviour* (Cambridge).

Jewkes, J., Sawers, D. and Stillerman, R. (1958), *The Sources of Invention.*

Jones, R. and Marriott, O. (1970), *Anatomy of a Merger: the History of G.E.C., A.E.I. and English Electric.*

Kalecki, M. (1945), 'On the Gibrat Distribution', *Econometrica.*

Kapteyn, J.C. (1903), *Skew Frequency Curves in Biology and Statistics* (Groningen).

Kerr, W.A. (1949), 'Labour Turnover and its Correlates', *Journal of Applied Psychology.*

Khalilzadeh-Shirazi, J. (1974), 'Market Structure and Price-cost Margins in U.K. Manufacturing Industries', *Review of Economics and Statistics.*

Kilpatrick, R.W. (1967), 'The Choice among Alternative Measures of

Industrial Concentration', *Review of Economics and Statistics.*

Kleiman, E. (1971), 'Wages and Plant Size: A Spillover Effect', *Industrial and Labour Relations Review.*

Knight, A. (1972), 'Economies of Scale', (paper read to the *Manchester Statistical Society*).

Kolm, S.C. (1969), 'The Optimal Production of Social Justice', in J. Margolis and H. Guitton (eds.) *Public Economics.*

Kuehn, D. (1975), *Takeovers and the Theory of the Firm.*

Lester, R. (1967), 'Pay Differentials by Size of Establishment', *Industrial Relations.*

Lintner, J. and Butters, J.K. (1950), 'Effect of Mergers on Industrial Concentration, 1940–47', *Review of Economics and Statistics.*

Lipsey, R.G. (1963), *An Introduction to Positive Economics.*

Little, I.M.D. and Rayner, A.J. (1966), *Higgledy Piggledy Growth Again* (Oxford).

Lothian, Lord (1930), article in *Manchester Guardian*, 8 January 1930, as quoted in Tawney (1964), p. 171.

Lucas, A.F. (1937), *Industrial Reconstruction and the Control of Competition.*

Luce, R.D. and Raiffa, H. (1957), *Games and Decisions* (New York).

Manne, H. (1965), 'Mergers and the Market for Corporate Control', *Journal of Political Economy.*

Marshall, A. (1890), *Principles of Economics* (1st edition).

Marshall, A. (1891), *Principles of Economics* (2nd edition).

Marx, K. (1887), *Capital* (page references to the translation from the Third German Edition by Moore and Aveling, edited by Dona Torr, 1946).

Mason, E.S. (1957), *Economic Concentration and the Monopoly Problem* (Cambridge, Mass.).

Masters, S.H. (1969), 'An Interindustry Analysis of Wages and Plant Size', *Review of Economics and Statistics.*

Mayer, C.P. (1976), 'Share Prices, Growth and Mergers' (unpublished B.Phil. thesis, Oxford).

Meehan, J.W. and Duchesnau, T.D. (1973), 'The critical level of concentration', *Journal of Industrial Economics*

Meeks, G. (forthcoming), *Disappointing Marriage: A Study of the Gains from Merger.*

Merton, R.K. (ed.) (1952), *Reader in Bureaucracy* (Glencoe, Illinois).

Metcalf, D. and Nickell, S. (1975), 'Monopolistic Industries and Monopoly Profits', LSE mimeo.

Monopolies Commission (1969), *Unilever Ltd and Allied Breweries Ltd* (H.C. 297).

Monopolies Commission (1973), *British Match Corporation and Wilkinson Sword* (cmd. 5442).

Moodies (1976), *Share Price Index.*

Nelson, R.L. (1959), *Merger Movements in American Industry 1895–1956* (Princeton).

Nettl, J.P. (1965), 'Consensus or Elite Domination: the Case of Business', *Political Studies.*

Newbould, G.D. (1970), *Management and Merger Activity*, (Liverpool).

Newbould, G.D. and Jackson, A. (1972), *The Receding Ideal* (Liverpool).

Niehans, J. (1958), 'An Index of the Size of Industrial Establishments', *International Economic Papers.*

Niskanen, W.S. (1973), *Bureaucracy – Servant or Master?*

Payne, P.L. (1967), 'The Emergence of the Large Scale Company in Great Britain 1870–1914', *Economic History Review.*

Peacock, A.T. and Wiseman, J. (1961), *The Growth of Public Expenditure in the United Kingdom.*

Penrose, E.T. (1959), *The Theory of the Growth of the Firm* (Oxford).

Pigou, A.C. (1947), *Aspects of British Economic History 1918–1925.*

Polti, R. (1974), 'Italy', (in R. Vernon (ed.) *Big Business and the State*).

Prais, S.J. (1957), 'Financial Experience of Giant Companies', *Economic Journal.*

Prais, S.J. (1974), 'A New Look at the Growth of Industrial Concentration', *Oxford Economic Papers.*

Prais, S.J. and Reid, C. (1974), 'Large and Small Manufacturing Enterprises in Europe and America', NIESR paper prepared for *Second International Conference on the Economics of Industrial Structure* Nijenrode, 1975 (published) 1976 eds, A.P. Jacquemin and H.W. de Jong).

Pratten, C.F. (1970), 'A Case Study of a Conglomerate Merger', *Moorgate and Wall St.*

Pratten, C.F. (1971), *Economies of Scale in Manufacturing Industry* (Cambridge).

Pratten, C.F. and Dean, R.M. (1965), *The Economies of Large-scale Production in British Industry* (Cambridge).

Pryor, F.L. (1972), 'An International Comparison of Concentration Ratios', *Review of Economics and Statistics.*

Quandt, R.E. (1966), 'On the Size Distribution of Firms', *American Economic Review.*

Reader, W.J. (1970), *Imperial Chemical Industries: A History*, vol. 1.

Reader, W.J. (1975), *Imperial Chemical Industries: A History*, vol. 2.

Reddaway, W.B. (1972), 'An Analysis of Take-overs', *Lloyd's Bank Review.*

Reed, A. (1973), *Britain's Aircraft Industry.*

Rees, G. (1969), *St. Michael: A History of Marks and Spencer.*

Revans, R.W. (1958), 'Human Relations, Management and Size', in E.M. Hugh-Jones (ed.) *Human Relations and Modern Management* (Amsterdam).

Rothschild, M. and Stiglitz, J.E. (1970), 'Increasing Risk I: A Definition', *Journal of Economic Theory.*

Ryden, B. (1972), *Mergers in Swedish Industry* (Stockholm).

Sampson, A. (1965), *Anatomy of Britain Today.*

Samuel, R. (1960), 'Bastard Capitalism', in E.P. Thompson (ed.) *Out of Apathy.*

Samuels, J.M. (ed.) (1972), *Readings on Mergers and Takeovers.*

Samuels, J.M. and Smyth, D.J. (1968), 'Profits, Variability of Profits and Firm Size', *Economica.*

Sawyer, M.C. (1971), 'Concentration in British Manufacturing Industry', *Oxford Economic Papers.*

Scherer, F.M. (1970), *Industrial Market Structure and Economic Performance* (Chicago).

Scherer, F.M. (1973), 'The Determinants of Industrial Plant Sizes in Six Nations', *Review of Economics and Statistics.*

Select Committee on Expenditure (1972), *Public Money in the Private Sector.*

Servan-Schreiber, J.J. (1969), *The American Challenge.*

Shepherd, W.G. (1966), 'Changes in British Industrial Concentration, 1951–8', *Oxford Economic Papers.*

Shepherd, W.G. (1972), 'Structure and Behaviour in British Industries with U.S. Comparisons', *Journal of Industrial Economics.*

Shonfield, A. (1965), *Modern Capitalism: The Changing Balance of Public and Private Power.*

Shorey, J. (1975), 'The Size of the Work Unit and Strike Incidence', *Journal of Industrial Economics.*

Shubik, M. (1959), *Strategy and Market Structure* (New York).

Silberston, Z.A. (1972), 'Economies of Scale in Theory and Practice', *Economic Journal.*

Simon, H.A. and Bonini, C.P. (1958), 'The Size Distribution of Business Firms', *American Economic Review.*

Singh, A. (1971), *Take-overs, Their Relation to the Stock Market and the Theory of the Firm* (Cambridge).

Singh, A. (1975), 'Takeovers, "Natural Selection" and the Theory of the Firm', *Economic Journal.*

Singh, A. and Whittington, G. (1968), *Growth, Profitability and Valuation* (Cambridge).

Singh, A. and Whittington, G. (1975), 'Size and Growth of Firms', *Review of Economic Studies.*

Steindl, J. (1965), *Random Processes in the Growth of Firms.*

Steiner, P. (1961), 'Monopoly and Competition in Television: Some Policy Issues', *Manchester School.*

Stigler, G.J. (1956), 'The Statistics of Monopoly and Merger', *Journal of Political Economy.*

Stigler, G.J. (1968), *The Organisation of Industry* (Homewood, Illinois).

Stoikov, V. and Raimon, R. (1968), 'Determinants of Differences in Quit Rate among Industries', *American Economic Review.*

Suetonius, G.T. (120), *Lives of the Caesars* (Rome).

Sutherland, A. (1969), *The Monopolies Commission in Action* (Cambridge).

Talacchi, S. (1960), 'Organisational Size, Individual Attitudes and Behaviour: An Empirical Study', *Administrative Science Quarterly.*

Tawney, R.H. (1964), *Equality* (5th edition).

Telser, L.G. (1972), *Competition, Collusion and Game Theory.*

Theil, H. (1967), *Economics and Information Theory* (Amsterdam).

Trades Union Congress (1902–75), *Report of the Annual Trades Union Congress.*

Utton, M.A. (1971), 'The Effects of Mergers on Concentration: U.K. Manufacturing Industry, 1954–65', *Journal of Industrial Economics.*

Utton, M.A. (1974), 'On Measuring the Effects of Industrial Mergers', *Scottish Journal of Political Economy.*

Vaizey, J. (1958), 'The Brewing Industry', in P.L. Cook and R. Cohen (eds.) *Effects of Mergers.*

Weber, M. (1948), *From Max Weber: Essays in Sociology* (edited by H.H. Gerth and C.W. Mills).

Weiss, L. (1966), 'Concentration and Labour Earnings', *American Economic Review.*

Weiss, L. (1971), 'Quantitative Studies of Industrial Organisation', in M.D. Intriligator (ed.) *Frontiers of Quantitative Economics* (Amsterdam).

Weston, J.F. (1953), *The Role of Mergers in the Growth of Large Firms* (Berkeley).

Weston, J.F. and Manshingka, S.K. (1971), 'Tests of the Efficiency Performance of Conglomerate Firms', *Journal of Finance.*

Whittington, G. (1972), 'Changes in the Top 100 Quoted Manufacturing Companies in the United Kingdom 1948 to 1968', *Journal of Industrial Economics.*

Wiles, P.J.D. (1952), 'Pre-war and War-time Controls', in G.N.D. Worswick and P.H. Ady (eds.) *The British Economy 1945–1950* (Oxford).

Wilkinson, E. (1939), *The Town that was Murdered.*

Woodward, J. (1958), *Management and Technology.*

Young, S. and Lowe, A.V. (1974), *Intervention in the Mixed Economy.*

Index